A CARE MANIFESTO FOR THE EARLY YEARS

The Need for an Ethic of Care in Childcare Policy and Practice

Zoë Raven

P

First published in Great Britain in 2026 by

Policy Press, an imprint of
Bristol University Press
University of Bristol
1–9 Old Park Hill
Bristol
BS2 8BB
UK
t: +44 (0)117 374 6645
e: bup-info@bristol.ac.uk

Details of international sales and distribution partners are available at policy.bristoluniversitypress.co.uk

© Bristol University Press 2026

DOI: 10.51952/9781447377382

British Library Cataloguing in Publication Data
A catalogue record for this book is available from the British Library

ISBN 978-1-4473-7735-1 hardcover
ISBN 978-1-4473-7736-8 paperback
ISBN 978-1-4473-7737-5 ePub
ISBN 978-1-4473-7738-2 ePdf

The right of Zoë Raven to be identified as author of this work has been asserted by her in accordance with the Copyright, Designs and Patents Act 1988.

All rights reserved: no part of this publication may be reproduced, stored in a retrieval system, or transmitted in any form or by any means, electronic, mechanical, photocopying, recording, or otherwise without the prior permission of Bristol University Press.

Every reasonable effort has been made to obtain permission to reproduce copyrighted material. If, however, anyone knows of an oversight, please contact the publisher.

The statements and opinions contained within this publication are solely those of the author and not of the University of Bristol or Bristol University Press. The University of Bristol and Bristol University Press disclaim responsibility for any injury to persons or property resulting from any material published in this publication.

Bristol University Press and Policy Press work to counter discrimination on grounds of gender, race, disability, age and sexuality.

Cover design: Nicky Borowiec
Front cover image: Carrie Wilks

Dedicated to Sophie, Imogen, Jolyon and Tris (my fab four)

Contents

List of figures, tables and vignettes		vi
Acknowledgements		vii
Preface		viii
1	Why a care manifesto is needed for the early years sector	1
2	Do governments care? The problem of marketisation	16
3	Can an organisation care?	33
4	Care ethics in childcare practice	46
5	Caring as an embodied practice in early years provision	62
6	Creating caring environments	80
7	Ethical sensemaking and how individuals can make a difference	93
8	Making childcare sustainable: a care manifesto	112
References		121
Index		135

List of figures, tables and vignettes

Figures
5.1	Hamington's aspects of embodied care	68
6.1	TV toy advertising: for boys and girls	89
7.1	Ethical sensegiving model, based on a model of organisational sensemaking	95
7.2	Embodied ethical sensemaking in early years practice	109
8.1	The three circles of sustainability	114

Tables
3.1	Applying a care ethics framework to the entrepreneurial process	38
4.1	Ethics of care theorists	50
4.2	Early years theorists	61
7.1	Typology of sensemaking in early years settings	96

Vignettes
2.1	Wet flannel training	26
6.1	The wrong scissors	86
7.1	Kieran's induction for a new member of staff	98

Acknowledgements

This book would not have been possible without the support and encouragement of my colleagues at Acorn Early Years Foundation, both in the action research team and across the organisation, including my wonderful board of trustees. I'd particularly like to thank Eva Lloyd and Narendra Laljani for their support and encouragement. My university supervisors, Anica Zeyen and Laura Spence, were also very encouraging – 'save that for your book' were words I heard many times during my doctoral journey! I'd also like to thank the team at Policy Press for giving me the opportunity to publish this book, and the reviewers of my book proposal for the insightful feedback.

I have so many sector colleagues that I would love to thank, but in the interests of confidentiality, I will not name any of them here – you know who you are, and if you read the book, you will no doubt recognise your own words! I have quoted verbatim from my research interviews and only changed details in the interests of ensuring confidentiality for all. I am so grateful for the generous gift of your time, and I'd particularly like to thank those who also helped to facilitate further interviews with their colleagues. Time is precious, and I was fortunate to be welcomed by a fantastic range of inspirational role models of caring early years practice.

I am also immensely grateful to my friends and family, especially my four wonderful children – two of whom have completed their own doctoral journeys. My parents would have been thrilled by my having a book published, and I owe them thanks for being the source of my determination to find ways of putting ethical ideas into practice as well as for encouraging my move into the early years sector. My dad, unwittingly, also gave me an insight into the ethics of care when I became a reluctant but dutiful carer for him in his final years. Finally, the arrival of my beautiful grandchildren spurred me on to complete this, renewing my fascination with early childhood development and confirming my conviction of the importance of nurturing care.

Preface

When I had my first child, in 1987, I was a secondary school English teacher. My parents ran an educational supplies business that had grown from my father's toy shop in Wellingborough, where my mother was running a preschool playgroup and struggling to find the kinds of toys and equipment that were robust and suitable for open-ended play. My mother expanded the playgroup into a day nursery and, after several years, she handed it over to the local community and joined my father in the business of supplying nurseries, playgroups, infant schools and special needs schools. When they created their first catalogue, it was noteworthy (at that time) for being a mainstream catalogue that, at my mother's insistence, included images of children with Down's syndrome and other special needs. I grew up with copies of *Nursery World* on the breakfast table and listening to conversations about childcare and early childhood development as well as hearing about my mother's role as a county chair in what was then called the Pre-School Playgroups Association.

The accepted thinking of the time was that attending a nursery or preschool was only really of benefit to children over two years old, and there was a lingering stigma around working mothers and the idea of placing babies and toddlers in day nurseries. My plan, then, when I had my first child, was to be a stay-at-home mum while she was little. I hadn't anticipated the boredom and frustration of caring for a baby while living in a rural location without a car. When my headteacher offered me the opportunity to return to work part-time, I jumped at the chance. My mother and a friend helped out with childcare, which worked for a while, but I soon realised that I needed something more consistent than mum taking Sophie with her to play in the Raven Educational Supplies showroom!

At this point, my father was supplying several schools and nurseries in the Milton Keynes area, so I asked him to recommend the best ones, as he'd visited them all (there were only a handful at that time). I then did my own visits, and my heart sank. Not only were they going to cost a significant proportion of my salary, but I couldn't see myself leaving Sophie in any of them. I complained to my parents that none of them felt homely and caring in the way Mum's had been, and I wasn't impressed with the array of cheap plastic toys that I saw (my parents had been champions of Community Playthings' wooden equipment from the start). My father's gruff comment 'well, if you think you know what a nursery should be like, why don't you open your own?' made me laugh – then it made me think. As a teenager, we had lived above my mum's nursery, which took up the ground floor and an extension of a large Victorian house in Wellingborough. I had liked having the space the nursery rooms provided at weekends, when we could move all the furniture out of the way and make room for me to practise my ballet and my brother to play table tennis. Maybe we could do something similar! In 1988, it turned out to be quite easy to persuade a bank manager to give us a very large mortgage to buy a converted Wesleyan chapel in the village of Castlethorpe, using the proceeds from our house sale as a deposit. There was space upstairs for three bedrooms, a bathroom and a living room, and we shared the kitchen downstairs with the nursery, which began with just 30 places for children aged 18 months upwards.

How the nursery developed into the Acorn Early Years Foundation is another story, but relevant to this book is the decision I made within a few months to add on a baby room in the Sunday school room that had been converted into a double garage, which became accommodation for six babies. The person who challenged my acceptance of the received wisdom about babies not benefiting from group day care was my second daughter, Imogen. At just a few months old, she had made it very clear that she much preferred crawling around among the older children in the nursery to spending quality one-to-one time with just her mum. Maybe, I thought, if we created a cosy space for just six babies with two members of staff to care for them, it would work. I still remember every child who began with us in the main nursery and every baby who joined us when we opened the baby room. We lived in the flat above the nursery for ten years, and I had two more children while we were there.

When I began the nursery, I was not trained in early years education and care, but I undertook a variety of courses and switched from teaching teenagers to training, assessing and mentoring the early years practitioners that formed my ever-growing staff team. The single nursery expanded into a group of nurseries (another story, and one which, bizarrely, sprang from my experience working as a breastfeeding counsellor with the National Childbirth Trust!). I immersed myself in the theories while also observing and participating in practice, and I particularly enjoyed working with those who had gained years of practical experience – as parents, childminders or nursery assistants – before working towards a qualification. Explaining concepts that they could then apply to familiar aspects of practice often felt like shining a light and revealing hidden gems. I particularly enjoyed working as an associate lecturer on foundation degree courses in early years and as an assessor on the Early Years Professional Status programme, seeing experienced, qualified practitioners develop into confident graduate leaders (before the ambition and funding for graduate leaders disappeared with a change of government).

Over the 36 years I have worked in the sector, I have become increasingly convinced of the importance of training and professional development for early years practitioners. I have also become increasingly concerned about the 'schoolification' that is infiltrating early years provision, treating early education as if it is simply preparation for school. Early years education is of crucial importance, but I feel strongly that care needs to come first. Children who are not emotionally and physically comfortable and secure cannot learn effectively. We are in danger of losing the fun and the warmth of caring early years practice in the obsession with measurable outcomes. What is worse is that children themselves are not being prioritised in a sector that is increasingly commercialised.

My intention in writing this book is to distil my thoughts about the problems being faced by the early years sector, coming from the unashamedly personal perspective of my own experience but also using six years of doctoral research. I draw on conversations and interviews with a wide range of practitioners, nursery managers and sector leaders. My focus is broad in that I examine the micro level of practice within nurseries as well as reviewing the macro level of government policy and societal influences. My aim is to identify the factors that influence whether early years care and education is provided in an ethical way. By ethical, I mean that while good quality is essential, provision should also be accessible, affordable and inclusive – and non-exploitative. We live in a society that is increasingly polarised, with deepening levels of inequality. Universal early years provision is not a panacea, but early childhood is the seedbed for adult life, and if we don't nurture our children with sufficient care, we are failing to prepare them for a fast-changing world.

The sector is facing huge challenges, but there are also opportunities and much to celebrate, and I owe a debt of gratitude to all my colleagues, both within my own organisation and across the sector. Acorn Early Years has now developed and grown from a single home-based nursery to a medium-sized group across three counties, and it has moved from a private company to a charitable social enterprise. Inevitably, this book is based on the experiences of myself and my colleagues during that journey, and where I refer to aspects relevant to Acorn, I clarify this is the case.

1

Why a care manifesto is needed for the early years sector

Introduction

When parents plan to return to work after maternity or paternity leave and are choosing a day nursery to look after their baby or toddler, their priority – other than the practical issues of affordability and the logistics of opening hours and accessibility – is to find a nursery that they feel confident will care for their child and practitioners who will offer a professional kind of love (Page et al, 2013). Parents and carers rightly expect nurseries to provide safe spaces and practitioners to be competent and caring. Their judgement, on visiting a nursery, will inevitably be influenced by what they see and what they are told about the nursery, and word-of-mouth recommendations are often a nursery's main source of enquiries. Reputations matter, and review sites are often as important as inspection reports. In England, which is the main focus of this book, inspections are carried out by Ofsted, the government department responsible for standards in education. Inspection reports can be over five years old, but their judgements remain influential if they are 'outstanding' or less than 'good' under the current system.

Parents selecting nurseries often describe the 'feel' of a nursery, which can include the sensory experience of its decor, light, space and smells, but most often they comment on the friendliness and demeanour of the staff they encounter and whether the children appear to be happy and engaged in activities. Whether practitioners come across as caring is a critical factor for most parents, although some may have educational outcomes as their main concern. Both the government and the early years sector itself spend more time focusing on early education than on care, and in this book I explore why that is problematic and argue for a resetting of priorities. To do so, I need to explain how this situation has arisen and the context of wider problems facing the sector.

The benefits of high-quality care and education in early childhood are widely recognised. There may be some debate about definitions of quality, 'a complex and multi-dimensional concept that is difficult to assess' (Organisation for Economic Co-operation and Development – OECD, 2025, p 24), but there is a general consensus about the features of high-quality education and care, which I explore later. The early years sector in the UK is, however, currently struggling with a triple crisis. First, underfunding over many years has contributed to ongoing problems with affordability, sufficiency and recruitment, particularly in areas of social disadvantage. Second, the level of qualifications held by those working in the sector is declining, reflecting a lack of understanding of the importance of high-quality early years practice, and this is jeopardising quality. Third, widespread 'schoolification' (OECD, 2006) valorises education at the expense of care, treating early years provision as simply a preparation for school. The lack of recognition of the work of early years practitioners reflects a wider undervaluing of care by society and a lack of understanding of the complexities of childcare practice. This book is following in the footsteps of *The Care Manifesto* by the Care Collective (Chatzidakis et al, 2020), and I hope to inspire the early years sector to adopt an ethic of care. In explaining why and how some parts of the sector have lost a focus on child-centredness, I explore the wider factors involved, from the macro world of government policy to organisational features, and then the micro world of childcare practice, and I focus on how ethical sensemaking can help to embed a care ethic in practice.

Where and how we lost the way (a quick history lesson)

Losing the way perhaps suggests that we were once in a better place, but my suggestion is that we have taken a wrong turn in an otherwise positive journey away from the stereotypical family structure of past generations, of working fathers and stay-at-home mothers. Women have had to fight for the right to have rewarding careers in a variety of sectors rather than being forced to become housewives (in itself an interesting term, suggesting marriage to a household). If careers are not to be prematurely curtailed or hampered by a long break, parenthood inevitably brings the challenge of childcare provision. I do not wish to denigrate the choices of parents who prefer not to take on paid work during their child's formative years, but this book explores the situation faced by families where parents want to continue with their careers while their children are young and by those parents who cannot afford not to work.

The first wrong turn was perhaps the (gradual) increase in maternity leave and maternity pay being limited to mothers. The increase itself is of course laudable, and there has been a noticeable reduction in the number of babies starting nursery before nine months as a result. Paternity leave, however, is woefully inadequate in the UK, and equal parenting would be easier to achieve if fathers were enabled and encouraged to share the responsibility and care for babies in the critical early months. This isn't solely an issue for parents in the UK, as Peter Moss and Linda Mitchell have clearly summarised in their overview of early childhood in the Anglosphere (Moss and Mitchell, 2024).

I suggest another wrong turn is the inexorable rise in nursery opening hours, although this has been offset in many ways by an increase in part-time places. The increase in demand for part-time places has come about partly because of the gradual decline in average working hours in the UK over many years. Similarly, the introduction of the right to request flexible working has resulted in a decrease in the proportion of children attending nurseries full-time. The increase in part-time places also reflects many families' need to reduce the cost of nursery fees by relying on unpaid family support for part of the week. In terms of extended hours, there are clearly benefits for parents whose working hours do not comply with standard office hours. However, the impact of both more part-time places and extended hours on both children and practitioners is that there is inevitably a reduction in continuity of care as a result, and increased pressure on early years practitioners to work very long hours.

Some years ago at Acorn Early Years Foundation (a charitable social enterprise providing early care and education that I started as a single nursery in 1989), we reduced our closure weeks to ensure that we were offering a comparable service to nurseries that were open all year round, closing only for public holidays. This change was short-lived. We were surprised by the number of parents who expressed their disappointment, arguing that they felt it was important for the whole nursery team to have a break but also that it enforced family time for themselves – for example, employers couldn't insist on their working between Christmas Day and New Year if they could honestly say that their child's nursery was closed. After much discussion, we came to the conclusion that although the closure (for the working days between these public holidays) would be expensive, as we would have no income to cover the overheads for that period, the benefits of having a closure period that everyone could enjoy at the same time would justify it in terms of employee well-being and avoiding the stressful negotiations about who would have to work over the holiday period. We also realised it would offer managers a time in which to truly relax without worrying whether their nursery is coping without them.

The most significant wrong turns, however, I suggest, are twofold. First, early education has been valorised over the practice of care. 'Schoolification', as it has been called (OECD, 2006), describes an over-emphasis on children's 'school-readiness', but early childhood care and education (ECCE) is so much more than a preparation for compulsory schooling. When the responsibility for inspecting day nurseries passed from social services departments to Ofsted in 2001, it was very evident which inspectors had an education background and which were more familiar with the welfare focus of social services inspections. Despite the inspectors having been trained to ensure consistent criteria in inspections, my colleagues and I found that those who had previously only inspected schools and preschool age groups (three- and four-year-olds) were often less interested or lacked confidence in assessing the provision for babies. The launch of the Birth to Three Matters framework two years later was very much welcomed by the sector, as it embraced a holistic approach to child development, which was in danger of being subsumed by the focus on preparing children for school. The guidance was produced 'by the sector, for the sector' and was seen by many as a way of standing up for a more child-focused approach than the goal-focused Early Years Foundation Stage framework. The hierarchy of ages, however, which reflects the hierarchy within the wider education system, is still present. When the introduction of Early Years Professional Status (since replaced by Early Years Teacher Status) led to more graduates in nurseries, it was noteworthy that few were based with the youngest children in nurseries, reflecting the prevailing belief that it was the preschool age group that most needed the more highly qualified early years professionals.

Second, arguably the biggest wrong turn has been in the neoliberal reliance on marketisation to develop the early years sector. I cover this in more detail in the next chapter, but an increasing reliance on market forces has led to a commodification of childcare and the growth of large corporate chains, often equity funded by multinational investment companies. Nurseries have grown larger, and the traditionally dominant small private and voluntary settings have been increasingly unable to compete, lacking the benefit of economies of scale. Maintained nursery schools and local authority nurseries, funded directly by the state ('supply side' funding), have also been in decline, despite nursery schools being simultaneously held up as beacons of high-quality early years education, and the recent policy to open more nurseries on school sites is already proving to be problematic in its implementation.

What's in a name?

Words matter, and the influence of terminology is often subconscious. The word 'mothering', for example, has very different connotations to 'fathering' – to mother a child suggests caring, whereas to father a child simply refers to an act of procreation. I discuss the gendering of childcare in Chapter 4, but in the early years sector, the evolution of terminology illustrates ongoing efforts to shift societal perceptions of childcare. As is common in any sector, early years professionals share a vocabulary – about both pedagogy and practice – but some terms are more contested than others, particularly those referring to professional roles in the sector. The National Nursery Examination Board qualification (known commonly as the NNEB) was used for a long period of time as a reference for what were usually termed 'nursery nurses'. The association of infant care with nursing stems from the welfare origins of childcare, and a small minority of nurseries (often those attached to private schools) still have 'matron' as a job title for those in charge. The term 'nursery nursing' is now rarely used in the sector. The standard early years qualification is now termed the Early Years Educator qualification. Some early years providers have campaigned for the use of the term 'teachers', in an attempt to raise the status of early years qualifications, but in this book I adopt the terms 'practitioner' and 'early years professional' to refer to the adults working in early years settings, as I feel 'educator' reinforces the emphasis on education, disregarding the role of caring. 'Pedagogue' is another problematic term in England as it has different associations (that is, being strict or pedantic) to the use of the term in Europe, where it has more holistic connotations.

Organisations have seen similar name changes. The Pre-School Playgroups Association, which was set up in 1961 and gained charitable status in 1963, changed its name to the Pre-School Learning Alliance in 1995 to switch the emphasis from 'play' to 'learning'. Their trading name is now the Early Years Alliance, reflecting a widening of their remit to represent all types of early years provision, not just the traditional sessional preschools. 'Early years' is generally a preferred term in the sector, covering both care and education, although 'childcare' is still used by commercial organisations, which, tellingly, often refer to the sector as an 'industry'. Other contested terms include 'dropping off' and 'picking up'; although these activities are commonly seen as simply part of the daily routine, they are in fact important transitions for both parents and children. Suzanne Zeedyk (nd) suggests on her 'connected baby' website that 'partings and reunions' might be more helpful terms, signalling their significance for building a child's emotional resilience.

The government is perhaps the most conflicted in its use of terms, referring to the funded entitlement as 'early education' in some instances and 'childcare' in others, seemingly under the impression that these are two separate entities. Most contentious of all is the way in which, for many years, the UK government used the word 'free' to describe the funded hours of early education and childcare, when in fact the level of funding has often been significantly below the cost of provision. The reference to '15 hours' and '30 hours' of childcare in relation to that funding is also misleading, as this equates to weekly hours during term time only, yet most parents work year-round. 'Free 30 hours' is, therefore, deeply misleading for parents, who might justifiably expect this to cover three fifths of full-time childcare costs. Of most concern is the government's admission that 'free' hours do not include the cost of meals, snacks, consumables and some activities. This suggests that they believe it's possible to treat children (via their parents and carers) like consumers, expecting them to understand that they might experience their day at nursery differently depending on whether their parents have paid for so-called 'optional extras'. I discuss the funding issue in more detail in the next chapter, as it encapsulates the issue of care ethics at the level of national policy.

Throughout this book, I use 'early years' and 'childcare' as generic terms for ECCE – encompassing both early education and childcare. I use the word 'care' when discussing childcare practices which are specifically focused on a child's physical and emotional needs, rather than having an educative focus. The age range of 'early years' is commonly considered to be birth to eight years, but as children in the UK usually start school in the autumn term following their fourth birthday, the age range covered in this book is the first four years of a child's life. My research area is focused on day nurseries, which provide full day care for working families. Sessional early years education comprises preschools in the private and voluntary sectors, and a small number of maintained (state-funded) nursery schools or nursery classes within schools. The association of nursery schools with high quality is perhaps behind the current UK debate about reviving a supply-funded model for early years provision, with schools taking the lead, but how that will work for babies, toddlers and working families who need longer hours is less clear.

The terminology of gender is increasingly contested, and many earlier research documents refer to 'mothers' and 'maternal' in ways which now seem stereotypical and reductive. I discuss in Chapter 4 the challenge of addressing the gender imbalance in the workforce and in parental engagement, and for the sake of a smoother reading experience, I use the word 'gender' when discussing the imbalance in the workforce, which is predominantly female, even though I am aware that any comparison of the sexes is an inextricable mix of biological sex and social gender constructions (Fine, 2017). Again for the sake of fluency, I use the term 'parents' to include carers, who may be non-familial. 'Practice' is a word with multiple definitions, and 'early years practice' is commonly used to describe the actions and methods used by adults in early years settings to care for and to educate children, which are based on a generally accepted version of 'best practice' taught in vocational training courses and monitored and regulated by Ofsted. Practice is also sometimes contrasted with theoretical approaches, with 'in practice' referring to what really happens, as opposed to the ideal; this is about theory in use as opposed to theory espoused (Argyris and Schon, 1974).

I should also clarify what I mean by 'care', as this is itself a problematic term. I do not equate it with childcare, but embrace the widely used definition that was first formulated by Bernice Fisher and Joan Tronto in 1990 (p 40, emphasis in original):

> On the most general level, we suggest that caring be viewed *as a species activity that includes everything that we do to maintain, continue, and repair our 'world' so that we may live in it as well as possible.* That world includes our bodies, our selves, and our environment, all of which we seek to interweave in a complex, life-sustaining web.

The Care Collective emphasise in their manifesto (Chatzidakis et al, 2020) the need to recognise that interdependence is universal and that care is political as well as moral. It is this broad range of meanings that I ascribe to care in this book, so although I limit my discussion to the early years sector, I focus on the governance and management of organisations just as much as the practice of childcare by individuals.

At this point, I should perhaps also explain why I do not agree with Peter Moss in his choice of words when it comes to education and care – though I do agree with almost everything else that he has to say about the problems of neoliberalism. Moss chooses to use 'early childhood education' without care being mentioned, because he considers that education is the main purpose of early childhood services and that 'care, understood as an ethic, should be an integral and essential part of all education (and other public) services' (Moss, 2023, p 14) . I completely agree that every service should be 'inscribed with care' (Moss, 2023, p 14), but I feel strongly that the practice of care should be valued in its own right and its importance recognised. When a parent is looking for somewhere or someone to look after their child when they return to work after maternity or parental leave, 'education' is not a good descriptor of the main focus of the childcare practice within the baby room. Recent research found that '80% of the public could explain what "childcare" meant while only 23% could do the same for "early education"' (Early Education and Childcare Coalition, 2024, p 5).

Babies are supported to learn, all of the time, but practitioners are first and foremost caring for them. The undervaluing of care as a practice doesn't mean that we should abandon the term; rather, I argue, we should reclaim it and celebrate it. People can be highly educated and uncaring, and education can be delivered without care. I do understand why Moss and Dan Wuori, among others, argue forcibly for abandoning 'childcare' as a term (for example, Moss and Mitchell, 2024), but simply arguing that education should include care is, I believe, naive, ignoring the sad reality of what goes on in too many educational settings today. This is why the issue of schoolification is at the heart of my argument for an ethic of care to take centre stage in early years practice. Carol Garboden Murray defines care as 'an action, an attitude, and an ethic', which captures the practice of care, the will to care, and the moral code which underpins ethical care; this centres 'relationship and interdependence as the universal human condition and values the virtues of caring such as empathy, compassion, love and trust' (2021, p 7). I hope to explain why such an ethic of care needs to be given a higher priority throughout organisations within the early years sector. Having defended the use of 'care' as a term in early years, however, I confess to disliking the term 'day care', which is more prevalent in the US but is sometimes used in the UK as a catch-all term for any kind of childcare that provides care and supervision of young children for working parents.

My personal preference is to use 'early care and education' to capture both aspects of what needs to be provided within day nurseries, my focus in this book.

The problems of schoolification and commodification

There is an unfortunate emphasis in the UK on baseline assessment of very young children, who usually start formal schooling after their fourth birthday. The Early Years Foundation Stage framework in England covers the age range from birth to five and has a very strong emphasis on learning and development, and measuring progress towards the early learning goals (Department for Education, 2025a). Widespread schoolification and a misguided emphasis on 'school-readiness' has resulted in a change of focus 'towards a staircase of pre-specified cognitive skills' (OECD, 2006, p 138), and despite the OECD pointing out that this has led to 'inadequate formulation of specific goals for the pre-school sector ... programme standards based on primary school criteria, and ... low levels of certification in early childhood pedagogy' (p 183), current UK policy appears to be continuing to encourage schools to extend their age range downward by opening nurseries in empty classrooms. Schoolification can lead to a neglect of the caring and nurturing dimension of early education due to the persistent hierarchy of education over care. This arises from a narrow view of both care and education as well as, it has been argued, the perspective of mind-body dualism (Van Laere et al, 2014). In Chapter 4, I discuss the Danish concept of *kropslighed*, as this offers an insight into how embodiment can be incorporated into pedagogy, recognising the importance of nurturing children's bodily and emotional development.

The valorisation of education over care reflects the widespread perception that caring for babies and children in the early years requires less qualifications or none, and it encourages the split system of care and education that prevails in the UK and much of Europe (Van Laere et al, 2012; Moss and Mitchell, 2024). While an integration of education and care has been successfully achieved in some of the Nordic countries, my research confirmed that the care and education of the very youngest children in the UK is very much the poor relation. The increased focus on cognitive and language development that is a feature of schoolification leads to the caring dimension of early years provision being overlooked or treated as almost an ancillary task compared to the more 'important' work of teaching and learning. When graduate qualifications were introduced to the UK early years workforce, I worked for a time as an assessor, and it was notable that baby room experience was almost always the area where candidates had to make additional arrangements to gain experience. And when qualified, almost all the graduate leaders that I encountered were placed either in the preschool room or in leadership positions. It was, and is, harder to find graduates working with babies and toddlers, despite that being such a critical period of a child's development.

Many early years writers and academics have tried, and are still trying, to persuade policy makers to take early years care and education more seriously, but one of my arguments in this book is that we are in danger of 'throwing the baby out with the bathwater' by rejecting 'care' as a descriptor for work in the early years. As noted earlier, some argue against using the term 'childcare', and June O'Sullivan of the admirable social enterprise London Early Years Foundation is adamant that early years professionals should be called 'teachers'. However, I disagree, because 'teaching' does not reflect the primary role of those in day nurseries. The assumption that care is part of education ignores the 'basic question of whether nurseries should be modelled on the intimacy and spontaneity of family interactions or the more professional and planned interactions of school' (Elfer, 2007, p 169). It also ignores the fact that 'care and education not only have different antecedents but have different underpinning ideologies arising from those different histories' (Sims, 2014, p 4).

'Pedagogy', an unfamiliar term for the general public in the UK, describes education that is more holistic, not simply focused on cognitive learning. The current hierarchy of learning over care implies that children require less 'care' as they get older; however, we all require care at different times throughout our lives, and an ethic of care, as I hope to demonstrate, would encourage a more compassionate and connected society. Education must not be reduced to cognitive development, and the focus on measurable outcomes and assessments, particularly prevalent in the UK, ignores the value and importance of care practices which offer a multitude of (unmeasurable) opportunities to nurture and develop our youngest citizens. 'Not everything that counts can be counted', as Einstein is purported to have said.

Another concern that is widely shared in the early years sector is the lack of understanding of the importance of play in early learning. The instinct to play is rooted deep in our nature, and the role of playfulness in creativity is at last being recognised within the adult world with impassioned pleas to allow children of all ages more opportunities for open-ended play and more freedom and to address the concerns that we are creating a generation that is in danger of 'forgetting how to play' (Bregman, 2020, p 288). Early years professionals understand the importance of play, but many parents and policy makers do not. At a meeting of parents from a nursery that Acorn were in the process of acquiring, one asked whether her child would be 'prepared for school'. I asked her what she meant by that, and she said: 'will she be able to write her name?' A brief explanation of our pedagogy ensued, but clearly there needed to be more engagement with parents at that nursery for them to understand how children learn and what the priorities need to be for a child facing the transition from nursery to school. There are a variety of types of play, and indeed our understanding of play has developed. For example, in the 20th century, Piaget suggested that children couldn't distinguish between fantasy and reality, but we now acknowledge that even very young children know that their imaginative play isn't 'real'. As Alison Gopnik explains: 'Pretending is closely related to another distinctively human ability, hypothetical or counterfactual thinking – that is, the ability to consider alternative ways that the world might be. And that, in turn, is central to our powerful human learning abilities' (2016, p 162).

Sadly, policy makers, even in the early years, do not always fully appreciate the importance of play, despite it being recognised as a right for children in the Convention on the Rights of a Child (United Nations, 1989). The Early Years Foundation Stage, a statutory framework for early years providers in England, emphasises learning, with play barely mentioned, although the *Birth to 5 Matters* guidance 'by the sector, for the sector' (Early Years Coalition, 2021) includes a clear explanation of how vital a child's right to play is.

Commodification of the sector is equally problematic, as I discuss in more detail in the following chapters. The current neoliberal hegemony has resulted in a reliance on market forces to provide sufficiency of provision and the misguided belief that competitive forces will also encourage high quality. In a nutshell, the issue is that children's care and education suffers from being treated as a consumer service, and the framing of parents as consumers ignores the complexity and importance of the triangular relationship between children and their familial and professional carers. Worst of all is the resulting perpetuation of social inequality, when high-quality provision is more readily accessible to those who can afford higher fees or the so-called 'optional extras'. Again, this is where an ethic of care is needed, not just to ensure that all children have access to high-quality provision, but also to rectify the exploitation of early years professionals, who typically treat their poorly paid employment as a vocation, perpetuating their role as one suitable for caring females rather than one which is critically important and which would benefit from a gender-balanced workforce that is highly valued and treated with the respect it deserves. In seeking to promote an ethic of care, we shouldn't focus purely on the educational aspect of the pedagogical role, but recognise that care is a 'deliberately *ethical* undertaking, motivated by a sociopolitical concern to "make a difference"' (Taggart, 2019, p 98, emphasis in original).

The research journey to solve an ethical problem

This book has had a long incubation: the ideas in it have been developed over 35 years. My original ambition was to explore whether and how high-quality, ethical childcare could be made financially sustainable as well as accessible and affordable to all. I had opened a small nursery and grown it into a small group of nurseries, and I had become increasingly disenchanted with the traditional business model, which focuses on profit and finding locations for nurseries within affluent areas. I wanted to discover how best to provide high-quality childcare in areas of deprivation, and my idealistic ambition underpinned my research questions, which were, specifically, about discovering the factors that facilitate or hinder the provision of ethical childcare. By 'ethical', I mean provision that is of high quality but also inclusive, affordable and non-exploitative. I transformed my group of nurseries, under the Acorn brand name, into a charitable social enterprise, as I wanted to test my theory that this is a more effective business model for ethical childcare provision. My decision to undertake a PhD was triggered by the experience of giving evidence to a House of Commons select committee about the policy to increase the number of funded hours (House of Commons Committee of Public Accounts, 2016). I was unimpressed by the research that apparently underpinned the then government's funding policies, and I was increasingly uneasy about the ongoing marketisation of the sector. I tried to discover the rationale behind the funding policies, and my reading led me to undertake my own research to discover the most effective way to provide high-quality early years care and education in an affordable, accessible and inclusive way.

My research stemmed from a relational ontology and epistemology, perhaps reflecting my immersion in the field of early learning, where social constructionism is a natural paradigm, emphasising the importance of sociocultural influences on children's development. I also drew on wide-ranging disciplines – philosophy, psychology and sociology, among others. A relational approach necessitates reflexivity and a moral awareness of the consequences of our words and actions, and this ethical emphasis was very appropriate for my research focus. It also naturally fed into a relational methodology, and I adopted a social constructionist perspective (Dachler and Hosking, 1995; Uhl-Bien, 2006), focusing on relational processes rather than the interrelations between individuals. This meant that my research focus extended beyond the words spoken in interviews to explore other forms of sociomaterial communication within settings. The risk of this approach is the difficulty of pinning down specific insights and conclusions – the concept of relational knowledge has been described as 'inescapably diffuse' (Eberle, 1995, p 212). However, I found that phenomenological analysis enabled insights into the development of organisational knowledge and culture and the relational dynamics of leadership and governance in early years settings.

When I started my research journey in 2016, while still working full-time, I quickly realised that there was a very real risk of my research having only a transitory value if I focused on government funding policies, which might suddenly change. Rather than concentrating on specific policies, I sought to examine the differences between organisations, and I knew that I had an extensive network within the sector which I could tap into. The focus on ethical childcare, and the factors that hinder or facilitate it, remained a constant theme, though after initially planning a meso-level study to look at organisational factors, I realised that I needed to look at all levels of influence, from macro to micro. On discovering the ethics of care, I realised its relevance and validity as a research lens, and a year later I began exploring practice theory as a way of drilling down into the detail of what ethical childcare means in practice, particularly in the care routines within nurseries. After disappearing down many rabbit holes in a range of research literature, I began to gather my own data in November 2019.

My research strategy was to conduct interviews across a range of roles and in a variety of early years settings. I initially intended to focus on a small number of organisations as representative case studies, but this strategy became problematic, due largely to the impact of the COVID-19 pandemic, so I switched to online interviews and extended the scope to a wider range of settings, including some within my own organisation. This also made it easier to guarantee confidentiality, as my source material covered a much wider range of settings and geographical areas than was originally planned. My inductive approach evolved into an abductive approach, as the iterative process of reading and re-reading my data led me back to the literature of sensemaking, which then informed the subsequent analysis. I spent 15 months interviewing a wide range of individuals, and my interpretation and analysis of the data ranged from the macro context to granular detail of practice as I examined the influences and factors that either hinder or facilitate the provision of high-quality, inclusive childcare, and what 'ethical' really means in day nurseries. It was easy to be interested in the fine detail of childcare practices as they have been part of my working life for many years, and discussing how others approach them led to insights into commonalities and differences between settings and the attitudes to care practices. I was acutely aware of my personal proximity to the research subject, but I also recognised that my immersion in the sector enabled me to understand my interviewees' perspectives and build a rapport with them. I remain enormously grateful for their time and thoughtful reflections.

When the COVID-19 pandemic brought my nursery visits and face-to-face interviews to an abrupt halt about halfway through my fieldwork, I continued them via Zoom and extended the range of interviewees, also including some nursery parents and external trainers and consultants. I completed 41 individual interviews and also gathered data via a focus group, which was helpful in adding more perspectives from practitioners, who had been difficult to schedule interviews with. In total, 53 people participated across 12 organisations. Interview data often included accounts of working in previous nurseries, so the examples included in the book do not necessarily come from interviewees' employment at the time of the research. Pseudonyms have been used to protect confidentiality, and ethical approval was given by my university, both at the outset and when a change of tactic was triggered by the pandemic. In taking a relational approach, I was acutely aware of my personal proximity to the research subject, but I felt strongly, and still do, that my involvement in the sector, and in one of the organisations included in the research, enabled me to access a wider range of individuals, ask more relevant questions and elicit more honest and detailed responses than would normally be possible. I successfully built on my sector connections and my knowledge and understanding of the issues being faced by practitioners and leaders. This pre-existing understanding helped me to establish rapport with interviewees and to develop greater insight into the dynamics and tensions reflected in the data by talking to and spending time with people in the research context (see Jones and Bartunek, 2021).

The data gathered for my research consisted of transcribed interviews, notes on informal observations, personal diaries and a range of information gathered from publicly available documents and social media. This included research conducted by other organisations with related interests and what is called 'grey' literature – material that is produced outside of academic and commercial publishing – such as reports and working papers produced by companies and voluntary organisations. I recorded and transcribed the face-to-face interviews, and the online interviews were recorded with video as well as sound, which enabled me to review facial expressions and body language. In many of my visits to different settings, I was given guided tours, which proved very helpful as I could ascertain the quality of practice, as I perceived it, from the interactions I witnessed between early years professionals and children, the physical environment, but also the body language, emotional atmosphere and staff behaviours, which illustrated the relationships between managers and their practitioners. Additional background research included examining Ofsted reports and company accounts as well as the participation of interviewees in sector issues, whether to do with funding or practice, via views expressed on social media and in published articles. I triangulated my data to examine whether there was consistency between the views expressed in interviews with me and interviewees' other statements and actions.

The 12 organisations that took part in my research were situated in a range of urban and rural locations across England, across areas with a range of demographic characteristics. They included three large providers, five small to medium nursery groups and four single-site nurseries, and the organisation types ranged from private for-profit companies to charitable social enterprises and family-owned and employee-owned nurseries and organisations. The nurseries themselves, as well as having different sizes, had different types of premises and varied in their longevity of operation. In fact, the range of settings discussed in the semi-structured interviews was even wider than the selected organisations, as many interviewees had worked at several different settings and were often keen to discuss the differences between the places they had experience with. My interviewees included founders and chief executives of large organisations, individuals in director-level roles, owners, managers and practitioners. Only 7 of the 41 interviewees were male, and 6 of them (unsurprisingly) were in leadership roles. Later additions to my dataset included parents who had experienced more than one nursery and two independent trainers and consultants, who both had extensive experience of observing practice in a range of settings.

In undertaking my analysis of the interview data, I found that sensemaking concepts, as well as reflecting my own research journey, helped to explain some of the findings. I hope that my research helps to fill a gap in the studies of this sector, which are usually situated in education and the field of organisation and business management. I also found insights in the increasingly multidisciplinary nature of my further reading, as I ventured into philosophy, sociology, neuroscience and psychology. Since completing my doctorate in late 2023, I have revisited the original data and accompanying diaries and journals, and in this book, I take advantage of the format to include a much wider range of personal reflections than was possible in my thesis.

Outline of the book

In this first chapter, I summarised my personal research journey and set out the issues facing the sector and the workforce, which I address in more detail in the rest of the book, offering some solutions. In Chapter 2, I explore the sector problems at a macro level, explaining why early years care and education is undervalued and considering why care is a problematic term, how marketisation has increased inequality and why schoolification is a problem. I examine the politics of care, tracing the influence of well-intentioned but often poorly executed government policies in the UK. I compare the unintended consequences of these policies and the underpinning problems of neoliberal hegemony with strategies implemented by other countries, and explore the role of learning and development as a change agent. In Chapter 3, I look at care practice at the organisational level and explore how transactional relationships and the influence of profit as a driver can have a negative impact on quality and inclusivity. I argue in Chapter 4 for an adoption of an ethics of care by the sector. The chapter begins with an explanation of the maternal roots of care ethics, how the concept has evolved and why gender is an important issue for the early years sector. I examine the ways in which an ethic of care can be applied in childcare practice and within the policies, pedagogy and daily routines of nurseries. I zone in further to consider the micro level in the fifth chapter, focusing on the embodied nature of caring practice and the role of tacit knowledge, emotions and pace. In Chapter 6, I examine the importance of sociomateriality in childcare settings and how the well-being of both children and practitioners is affected by the nursery design, furnishings and equipment, including the problematic nature of protective clothing.

I then consider ethical sensemaking in Chapter 7 as a way of embedding ethics in practice through sensemaking and sensegiving. I look at how this differs from ethical decision-making, the influence of leadership, organisational culture and levels of autonomy, and how to prevent ethical slippage. I conclude in Chapter 8 with a call for a (child)care manifesto, outlining how this could help to address the financial and environmental sustainability issues facing the sector. Care is presented as a political issue, and I argue there is a need to reset education priorities and to pay more attention to the youngest children and babies within nurseries. The need to understand, value and appreciate the embodied nature of childcare practices is a theme that runs throughout the book, and in setting out my (child)care manifesto, I highlight the opportunities for both the early years sector and society that a widespread adoption of an ethic of care offers.

2

Do governments care? The problem of marketisation

The triple policy agenda

The benefits of high-quality early childhood care and education (ECCE) have been recognised for many years, particularly for children living in areas of economic deprivation (Organisation for Economic Co-operation and Development – OECD, 2006; Allen, 2011; Tickell, 2011; Mathers et al, 2014), and the UK government has duly responded with increased public spending and a significant rise in policy attention. The two primary objectives have been: to improve child development in order to improve later outcomes and to increase maternal employment. These could be seen as education and childcare initiatives, respectively. They have also been described as part of a triple policy rationale, concerned with social mobility, economic well-being and social justice (Lloyd and Potter, 2014), and I examine each of these policy strands to consider whether and how they demonstrate an ethic of care on the part of the government of the day.

First, then, the rationale for ECCE as an aid to social mobility is that supporting children's socioemotional and intellectual development provides a foundation for better educational outcomes, and this will lead to better employment prospects. Indeed, ongoing research confirms this (Crowley et al, 2025). The provision of 'free' early education is intended to level the playing field for children starting school, but there is inequality in the access to high-quality provision and inevitably a limit to the effectiveness of the universal entitlement of 15 hours a week for 38 weeks of the year within the context of increasing poverty and inequality. Early education is not a panacea for the problems of inadequate housing and poor nutrition, and the extended '30 hours' of funding for childcare is only available to working families if they are able to demonstrate regular earnings at a certain level, and even then, not all of these families access this support. Research for the Early Education and Childcare Coalition shows that the families and children from more disadvantaged backgrounds, who are most likely to benefit from early care and education, are also the least likely to be able to access or use it (Hardy et al, 2022).

The second element of the triple policy agenda, economic well-being, recognises that the cost of childcare is the biggest single barrier to work for parents of young children (Save the Children, 2018). A survey by Pregnant

Then Screwed (2022) even shows that women's worries about childcare costs are a significant factor in their decision to have an abortion. The staged increases in funded hours and the extension to younger children means that in England, eligible working families of children aged 9 months to 4 years can claim funding for 30 hours a week, which has been welcomed by many, but this has proved to be both misleading and bureaucratic. The '30 hours' is in fact just over 22 hours if the funding is stretched across the year, which is typically the case as most parents do not work only in term time. The inadequate hourly rate for the preschool age group means that most families have to pay significantly higher rates for the remaining hours, as providers must compensate for the underfunding of the so-called 'free' hours. It is also puzzling to many that children in non-working families, who arguably are most in need of early years care and education, are entitled to fewer funded hours, and none at all in many cases. If parents work insufficient hours, or do not work, only two-year-olds deemed to be vulnerable are entitled to any funded hours, and three- and four-year-olds are limited to the universal entitlement of just 15 hours a week.

There has also been a low take-up of the tax-free childcare scheme, and the conditionality of the entitlement has led to some parents on zero-hours contracts finding themselves unable to access the scheme because they cannot demonstrate the regularity of their working hours, and to some parents losing their entitlement because they miss the deadline for revalidating their claim every three months. The inconsistency of funding across the four UK nations adds to the confusion and frustration.

Finally, the social justice aspect of the policy agenda is focused on reducing inequality by making childcare and early education more accessible, aiming to narrow the attainment gap and provide equal access to high-quality provision. This is where the dominance of a pay-as-you-go private market defeats the laudable intention. Freshly prepared nutritious meals do not form part of the funded entitlement, and in theory, parents can opt out of having to pay additional costs for meals or can choose sessions which do not include meals. The exclusion of some children from the social capital of the mealtime experience in a nursery is an example of non-inclusive provision, going against the ethos of most early years settings and reinforcing the inequality between children from different backgrounds. It is not just about the nutritional quality of the meals given to children, but also about their experience of learning to use cutlery, serve themselves, scrape their own plates and discuss the ingredients in a range of dishes. This is something denied to children whose families have opted for providing a packed lunch to avoid the additional 'voluntary' charge for a meal. This is an example of a lack of care at a macro level in failing to recognise the importance of the cultural capital of mealtimes and the likely consequence that children from lower-income families will miss out on nutritionally balanced meals.

Similarly, snack times in nurseries are usually offered on a 'rolling' basis, where children can choose when to go to sit at a table with other children to enjoy fresh fruit or other healthy snacks, in order to minimise the disruption to their play. Quite how that can be offered as an 'optional extra' is baffling. Of more concern for those of us wishing to offer ethical, inclusive provision is the idea that some children may be taken off to experience forest school activities but those whose families cannot afford to pay an additional fee would be left behind. One of the main drivers behind my personal decision to change Acorn business model to a charitable social enterprise was hearing from my forest school leaders about the experience of taking children from one of our nurseries in an area of deprivation for their first forest school session. Not only did the children appear to be awed and overwhelmed by the novelty of being in a woodland, but they struggled to walk over the forest floor, being unused to surfaces that weren't completely flat. Without our determination to encourage their play and learning to take place as much as possible in natural outdoor environments, those children could easily end up suffering from what Richard Louv (2005) calls 'nature deficit disorder'. Forest schools should not be limited to children in middle-class families, but that will be the unintended consequence of the UK government's funding policy at the time of writing.

There are underlying tensions between the three strands in the policy agenda, particularly in terms of whether women in particular are being coerced into going back to work after maternity leave instead of having the choice to spend longer at home with their children. One of my interviewees referred to a piece of research involving mothers returning to work, who all felt that 'they were rushed back to work' and that they would have preferred shorter hours but couldn't afford this economically. Whether the driver for returning to work is economic necessity or a return to a rewarding and satisfying career, a significant factor influencing a parent's happiness with their childcare arrangements and their work–life balance is their perception of the extent to which their child is benefiting from the nursery experience. The experience of feeling worried and guilty about leaving a child in nursery is a world apart from feeling confident in a child's enjoyment and their access to a wide range of educational experiences, especially the messy and adventurous play that is not as easily provided in many homes. Many, of course, will experience both extremes, and the emphasis of the neoliberal hegemony on parental choice sidesteps the issue of affordability. Nurseries that offer the full range of high-quality provision, with superb environments, freshly prepared meals, forest schools and a team of highly qualified early years professionals, are not likely to be the most affordable in an area. The apparent strategy of shifting responsibility for poverty away from the state and onto parents has been commented on by many in the early years sector (Simpson et al, 2015; Penn, 2017; Oppenheim and Milton, 2021), and the House of

Commons' own Education Committee has noted that 'the Government's flagship 30 hours childcare policy appears to be entrenching disadvantage' (House of Commons Education Committee, 2019, p 3). The reason for this is the way in which it embeds neoliberal marketisation into the sector, and despite having a Labour government in place as of 2024, there is no indication that this is likely to change. As the OECD (2025, p 17) observes, early years policies 'are well positioned to reduce inequalities', but to do so, universal policies need to be mixed with targeted support for vulnerable children and families facing participation barriers. There are some efforts towards that, but in the UK, there is still a reliance on the market to provide sufficient early years provision, and this is problematic for several reasons.

Why marketisation is problematic in the early years sector

In the context of the early years sector, neoliberalism is most clearly evident in the reliance on the market for the provision of early years care and education. Maintained nursery schools, directly funded in the same way as maintained schools, were set up more than a century ago, but their numbers have almost halved since the mid-1990s. They are an example of supply-side funding, but successive governments have adopted policies of demand-side funding, ostensibly to give parents more choice in their childcare choices. This funding model relies on free market economics and assumes that market forces will ensure sufficiency of provision and that competition will encourage high quality. It reduces the power of the state to control how nurseries operate and is based on a belief in consumer choice. Local authorities have limited control over the childcare settings in their area and are discouraged from directly funding and managing provision. There are, however, several serious concerns about commodification of the sector, and these range from a fundamental concern about early education and childcare being treated as a service economy to specific problems around privatised provision.

Where profit is the main driver, decisions about fee increases may be based on what the market will tolerate rather than a transparent calculation about how much is needed to cover the costs and generate a modest profit. Salaries may also be set according to the recruitment situation, with an inevitable preference for employees who will accept lower salaries, which may dilute the level of qualified staff to a minimum. If companies are on a trajectory of growth in order to sell and make a profit, investment decisions will inevitably be short-term, and may prioritise improving perceptions of the nursery over intangible investments in, for example, training and developing staff teams. In the next chapter, I explore other, less obvious, implications of prioritising profit over quality. I am, of course, generalising, which is not fair to the many nurseries that are run as private companies and focus on providing the best care and education possible. And, of course, removing the profit motive is not a panacea. Local authority nursery provision cannot always be relied on to be of consistently high quality. In an era of budget cuts, the services that would support local authority provision are likely to be severely limited, which has an inevitable impact on quality.

Criticism of the marketisation of the early years sector has been prevalent in early years academia since the 2010s (Penn, 2011; Lloyd and Penn, 2013; Roberts-Holmes and Moss, 2021; Simon et al, 2022), with many arguing that markets are inevitably inequitable. As Helen Penn remarks, 'for-profit care is often exploitative, and distorts or damages quality and equity of access' (2012, p 20). Tronto also argues that the market is inevitably ineffective in providing care due to 'its complexity, low rate of return, and labor-intensive nature' (2010, p 159). There are certainly considerations which inhibit competitive forces in the sector, such as the pressures involved in parental choice. Families may not be able to make informed decisions related to the quality of childcare provision, may be severely limited by issues of accessibility and affordability, and, once a child has settled in a nursery, may find it very difficult to complain or change provider. 'Emotional stickiness' (Gallagher, quoted in Roberts-Holmes and Moss, 2021, p 85) can arise for a variety of reasons, including a parent being unsure of the causes of their child's unhappiness and whether or not it is related to the quality of care in a nursery. They then face the dilemma of whether to risk potential further upset to the child by moving them to a different nursery.

Viewing parents as consumers is also problematic given that their 'choice' of childcare provider is in reality very limited and unlikely to be well-informed. The logistics of availability, accessibility and affordability mean that there may be little or no choice for low-income families, making the terminology of 'choice' very misleading and masking the underlying structural inequality of a marketised sector. Making assumptions about parental choice can also have the insidious consequence of transferring responsibility for making the right choice about childcare to families who realistically cannot rate the quality of care processes when they are not present to witness them, relying instead on what they see at the beginning and end of the day and their interactions with the early years professionals, Ofsted gradings, reputation, information supplied to them by the childcare setting and their child's demeanour and feedback, if they are old enough to give it. Research measuring parental satisfaction and comparing it with 'expert' evaluations of quality found a uniformity of parental satisfaction that was influenced as much by availability and affordability as it was by perceived quality, confirming that parents can never be the kind of rational consumers that effective markets require (Vandenbroeck et al, 2023).

Finally, one of the more insidious elements in the reliance on market forces in the childcare sector is the way in which this has added to the pressure on parents of small children to work long hours and increased the likelihood of children spending long days in nurseries without consistent caregivers. Three decades ago, 8 am to 6 pm was considered a long day, and longer hours were offered by very few nurseries – usually those attached to hospitals or similar institutions. The opening hours of day nurseries now are rarely shorter than that ten-hour day, with many offering the option of significantly longer days. There has also been a noticeable increase in part-time booking patterns, due largely to parents' demand for flexible working hours when they return to the workplace. The latter is undoubtedly positive for the work–life balance in families, but, conversely, marketisation has had consequences for the quality of childcare. For example, Bright Horizons, one of the largest childcare chains, has created a service that provides emergency childcare as an add-on. This encourages nurseries to provide short-notice sessions for children who have never been to that nursery before.

This, I would argue, is unethical in that it puts unfair pressure on parents and risks emotional damage to children by encouraging the use of alternative, unfamiliar childcare in the event of a breakdown in the family's usual arrangements. It is antithetical to the normal emphasis in early years provision on continuity of care and carefully managed transitions. Shorter working hours for parents and carers would enable a more equal division of caring responsibilities, and, indeed, it can be argued that 'it is our absurd culture of overwork that fuels people's need to escape into compensatory consumerism' (Segal, 2023, p 209). A caring economy would aim for sustainable growth that avoids the current reliance on unpaid carers within families, whether they are caring for children, the elderly or those of any age with additional needs.

It's not (just) about the money

In its most recent Starting Strong report, the OECD recommends that 'to ensure public funding promotes quality and equitable access, even with private ECEC [early childhood education and care] providers, policies should allocate funding conditionality to some criteria, monitor large for-profit players, and limit family costs. Funding allocation mechanisms should be used to steer recipients towards quality and equity' (OECD, 2025, p 11). In the UK, there is a widespread consensus that the funding levels for the 'free entitlement' for three- and four-year-old children falls short of the cost of provision, and there have been repeated calls from many organisations across the sector for the funding levels to be increased. However, Penn argues forcefully that providing more money within the current system is not the answer and that '[t]he problem is the financial structure of the childcare industry itself, and, without reforms, more money will only enhance the inequities of childcare provision' (2024, p 14).

The way funding is applied by different providers is often opaque, and, as mentioned earlier, because the advertised '30 hours' only covers term time, most parents and providers spread the funding over a full year, so it actually only covers just over 22 hours per week. Parents are often shocked, therefore, to discover that fees can still be unaffordable, particularly with more than one child in nursery and if they want to include so-called 'extras', such as meals, snacks and the full range of activities. The guidance does not allow providers to state their fees and then deduct the funding, which would be much easier to administer and more transparent for parents. Instead, the funded hours have to be shown as 'free', then the charge is shown for the remaining hours and 'optional extras'. When funding changes from term to term – which it inevitably does as each term has a different number of weeks – and funding is applied at an hourly rate, providers are faced with varying income levels, exacerbated by deductions for periods of absence by children (depending on the local authority's guidance, which itself can vary widely).

The confusion is not all of the government's making. A 2024 report from the IPPR (Institute for Public Policy Research) and Save the Children notes that 'there is an asymmetry of information between government and providers' and that many childcare businesses are reluctant to share details of their costs with government (Reed and O'Halloran, 2024, p 27). The report further states: 'With a small but significant and growing minority of private equity-backed chains drawing significant levels of profit from the system, that reluctance may yet grow' (Reed and O'Halloran, 2024, p 27). It recommends more transparency from government on the setting of funding rates, which is even more important given that, as the report states, the government is the purchaser of 80 per cent of the childcare hours provided. It also highlights the need to demand more openness from providers about costs.

When funding is applied in the most transparent way possible, which is the approach Acorn and many other providers take, parents can be shocked by the discovery that fees may rise as their child gets older. This is the opposite of how it should be. In the UK, for babies and toddlers under two years of age, the staff-to-child ratio is 1:3, whereas for three- and four-year-olds, it is 1:8 (even 1:13 at times, when there is a graduate leader in the team; Department for Education, 2025a). Given that salaries comprise around 75 per cent of overheads, you would expect this to be reflected in the fees. It is, but the funding levels for the older, preschool age range are so inadequate that providers have to charge proportionately higher amounts for non-funded hours. This is partly due to a historic trend in the sector wherein fees for older children are used to subsidise spaces for younger ones, as providers recognised that when parents first return to work after parental leave, their financial situation is often at its worst and affordability is a major issue. Some providers have even switched to charging the same hourly rate for all children, regardless of age.

More worryingly, there is no scope within the funding process to compensate providers adequately for the additional workload and costs associated with children who have additional needs, which might be social and economic needs as well as special educational needs and disabilities. This inevitably deters many providers from taking children with additional needs but also, as my research confirmed, children from very low-income families. Those children may arrive at nursery hungry and with inadequate clothing for outdoor play, and there may be a need for early years professionals to take time out for case conferences and meetings with various agencies in relation to these children. Troubled families often need support with parenting and may also require assistance to access funding and help for some of their social issues. For these families, nurseries are often less 'scary' than social services departments, which are themselves stretched to the point where they may only be able to deal with severe cases. This puts a huge burden on nursery managers and their teams, and the funding levels do not account for the extra support needed in these cases; there is some deprivation funding, but, understandably, this comes with limitations on how it can be spent, and that does not usually include additional staff time.

Frustratingly for the private and voluntary sectors, there is an unequal playing field whereby the funding given to maintained (state-funded) schools and nurseries is significantly higher than the funding organisations in these sectors receive. This allows maintained schools and nurseries to pay more generous salaries and, therefore, recruit and retain more highly qualified staff. However, they rarely cover the full day for working families, and the government policy in England of encouraging schools to open nurseries on their premises risks endangering an already fragile sector. It is ironic that marketisation is affecting the relationship between schools and nurseries. Because of the way funding is applied, there have been several cases of outstanding nurseries being forced to close because schools have taken over premises previously leased to independent operators. 'Wraparound care', which provides additional hours to supplement sessional care offered by schools and school nursery classes, may be a workable solution for school-aged children, but it should not be the go-to solution for children of nursery age, who need continuity of care throughout the day.

Finally, a non-financial issue that exposes a lack of care at government and societal levels, largely due to ignorance, is the lack of public understanding about the practice of childcare and early years education. My interviewees consistently expressed frustration with the public perception of childcare. For example, Sharon commented:

> I think the British public and, therefore, a lot of parents also think, you know, the cheapest childcare we can get the better, because actually

all they do is babysitting, whereas you pay £10 an hour to have your dog walked and you expect to get childcare for less than £4 an hour – it's outrageous.

A broadsheet newspaper that covered a government proposal to water down staff-to-child ratios captured a societal misconception about early years settings by referring to staff 'watching over' children, demonstrating a lack of understanding of how children are supported to learn through play and the extent of the care demands of infants and young children (Riley-Smith, 2021). Interviewees expressed frustration with the simplistic understanding of caring that such a comment suggests, as it 'obscures the complexity and the intellectual challenge of work with young children' (Goldstein, 1998, p 245). These views echo my own perception of the persistent undervaluing of the early years workforce.

The COVID-19 pandemic exacerbated the low morale in the early years workforce. The most common reason for wanting to leave the early years sector in one survey during the pandemic was '[f]eeling undervalued by government', with 77 per cent of respondents reporting this reason (Early Years Alliance, 2021, p 5), higher than the percentage reporting poor pay. Many in the early years sector felt taken for granted during the pandemic. As one survey respondent commented: 'The early years sector is to education what the care homes are to the NHS. We were left hung out to dry' (Early Years Alliance, 2021, p 11). The recognition for carers and health professionals seemed to be limited to the publicly funded services, ignoring the fact that many settings in the private and voluntary sector were caring for the children of those workers as well as children deemed vulnerable.

Within public sector education, there is a move to encourage business practices, which is often referred to as new managerialism, and one study looked at the ethical implications of this in a school setting (Edwards et al, 2023). This found that senior leadership teams often adopted a justice-based approach to ethics, prioritising good grades and equal treatment of pupils, whereas teachers in non-leadership roles preferred a feminist ethic of care approach, focused on relationships, the need to adapt to individual needs and the importance of a broader social education. In some ways, this can be seen to be echoed in the hierarchy of the early years sector, with a government emphasis (through Ofsted) on measurable learning outcomes and a workforce that would, I suggest, instinctively prefer to focus on the individual needs of children and their social and emotional development. This tension is most clearly seen in the schoolification issue, which can be simplified as whether the priority is to prepare children for school or to provide a more holistic approach that aims to develop children's ability to cope with every aspect of life in the modern world.

The role of learning and development

In 1919, Margaret McMillan, a pioneer of nursery schools in England, observed that '[n]ot long ago it was held by most people that any nice motherly girl would do as a nurse for little children', but in fact early years teachers are 'helping to make a brain and nervous system, and this work which is going to determine all that comes after, requires a finer perception and a wider training and outlook than is needed by any other kind of teacher' (1919, pp 171, 175). Early years care and education is still subject to the same gendered assumptions, but there is increasing recognition of the importance of high-quality training for early years professionals. Knowledge and skills have been recognised as a precondition for effective care (Fisher and Tronto, 1990), and there is widespread evidence of the link between high-quality provision and staff qualification levels (Nutbrown, 2012; Mathers et al, 2014; Melhuish and Gardiner, 2019).

The UK, however, lags behind other European countries in the requirements for qualifications to work in early years care and education, with a gradual decline in qualification levels in recent years. In stark contrast to Iceland, for example, where 'only those who have a master's degree from an accredited university may use the occupational title "playschool teacher"' (Einarsdottir, 2017, p 65), government policy changes in recent years have resulted in a watering down of qualifications requirements for early years practitioners. Just 50 per cent of early years practitioners in a setting are required to hold a full and relevant qualification, and even Level 2 qualifications (which can be gained in one year post 16) can be counted. The aspiration of the Blair/Brown Labour government to have a graduate leader in every early years setting was quietly dropped when funding for graduate qualifications was withdrawn by the subsequent Coalition government. Unlike the initiative in Ireland to aim for a graduate-led workforce by 2028, and those countries that already have a graduate-led workforce, the UK government has yet to reintroduce any funding or support to improve the level of qualifications. Worryingly, the focus of the UK government appears to be on making it acceptable for unqualified staff to be given a fast-track route to qualified status as a way of tackling the recruitment crisis (Department for Education, 2025b). Affordability of childcare for working families is seen as a high priority, and lowering qualification requirements is seen as one way to reduce the cost, perpetuating the status of the workforce as low-paid and undervalued. Financial pressures for early years settings have also led to increasing pay compression, with very little additional remuneration for highly qualified staff. This is significant as research has shown that access to training and career progression is a core element in successful retention of the workforce (Hardy et al, 2024).

The report for the Early Years and Childcare Coalition also emphasises the importance of continuing professional development (CPD; Hardy et al, 2022). Access to CPD varies greatly between organisations, with some only providing the minimum mandatory training, outside of working hours, and others closing their provision in order to provide training days for whole teams together (in the same way that schools do). The importance of CPD was borne out in the accounts of my interviewees, who were unanimous about the positive impact of in-service training opportunities. At Acorn, we have found that one of the main benefits of our training days is that whole staff teams can share the experience and immediately discuss the practicalities of implementing or adapting new ideas to their setting. Sinead, a nursery manager in a chain of nurseries, who had introduced a training day not long before we spoke, said: 'we're all buzzing before we even get there. It's a day out for us … you take so much in, and it's really nice, and it becomes a team-building day for us.' Several interviewees commented that training opportunities made staff feel valued, and unsurprisingly given the nature of the work in early years settings, practical workshops were particularly enjoyed and seen as relevant.

Cost is one of the main barriers to training, however – particularly when budgets are tight or when there is pressure to generate profits – and often the largest cost is in freeing up early years practitioners to attend courses. The alternative option to providing in-service training days, or providing cover to free staff up, would be to expect practitioners to attend training after work or at weekends. This approach clearly lacks care for employees, who often work long days, and it would mean that training opportunities discriminate against those who have caring commitments outside their normal working hours. Vignette 2.1 describes a session which demonstrates the advantage of whole-group learning and also exemplifies the connection between sensible knowledge and practice-based learning – that is, tacit knowledge that is gained from sensory experience (Strati, 2007).

Vignette 2.1: Wet flannel training

Cara, a nursery manager at a for-profit nursery with a strong emphasis on respectful care, provided a vivid example of an impactful training experience which took place during an informal discussion after her interview. She recounted a particularly successful training session that she had done with practitioners, where she separated them into two groups. She explained the task to the first group, out of earshot of the second group, who had been told just to sit passively. Then, each member of the first group took a cold wet flannel and thoroughly but quickly wiped clean one hand of a person in the second group, without explaining why or engaging in any discussion. They then left the room, returned with a warm wet flannel, and sat beside the same person, this time taking the time to massage and clean the other hand, explaining what they were doing in a soft and gentle tone.

Cara described this exercise as being more effective and long-lasting than any discussion would have been, with all the practitioners realising, in an impactful sensory way, the difference it makes to care routines when they are done with sensitivity and a caring attitude. The recipients commented that their hands felt different from each other afterwards, with some asking for their first hand to be given the caring treatment of the second, to make them feel more balanced.

There are numerous barriers to providing training and professional development within the early years sector, and several of these link directly to marketisation. When early years settings are primarily seen as business units, with profitability as the highest priority, there is inevitably a reluctance to invest in anything which does not have an immediate and demonstrable impact on the nursery's success. Several of my interviewees suggested that nursery owners and managers not only fail to recognise the benefits of training, but in some cases do not welcome the new ideas that are brought back. For example, Rachel, a nursery assistant, described going on a training course which encouraged her to introduce 'risky play' in the nursery, but then, when a few children scraped their knees jumping from a low bridge, the nursery manager banned risky play, despite the practitioners being convinced of its benefits. Rachel felt frustration at this and believed that the risky play was seen as not complying with the 'very structured' teaching environment, which was in place because it was seen as what the parents, as customers, expected. Several interviewees made disparaging comments about managers or practitioners deemed to be 'old school', by which they meant not complying with the most recent best practice, such as the best practice on planning topics, and therefore not aligning their practice to the interests of the children. Training appeared to be the key factor in determining whether practitioners were aware of developments in early years practice, and the availability of and encouragement to do training was seen as very variable between different nurseries.

Support for higher-level qualifications is also an area which varies widely between different providers and relates directly to the support, or lack of support, from government. Although it is widely recognised that workforce qualification levels are key in determining quality, recent research suggests that this is deteriorating (Archer and Merrick, 2020), and government policy in the UK has focused on sufficiency more than quality. As noted earlier, the aspiration of the Blair/Brown Labour government for every early years setting to have a graduate leader by 2017 was quietly shelved by the Coalition government when the Graduate Leader Fund was discontinued (Mathers et al, 2011). Several of my interviewees noted that some organisations were reluctant to encourage their staff to work towards higher-level qualifications due to a fear of losing them to an employer who could offer a higher salary, more appropriate for graduates.

There was also a divergence of opinion from my interviewees about the relative merits of different qualifications in the sector, and some concern was voiced about the practical abilities of some graduates. Ros, a consultant and trainer who had also worked as a senior lecturer on early years degree courses, commented:

> I don't think it's the qualification itself ... the only thing I think of, by going to study, which is different to [getting a] qualification, is that you can learn things at a deeper level. So I would say studying and understanding at a deeper level is important, not necessarily the qualification.

Liz, another experienced trainer and consultant, summed up the view of several others when she said:

> I think it depends on the quality of the qualifications, doesn't it? ... You can be in a situation where you've got somebody who's unqualified and somebody who's qualified and the unqualified practitioner might be better than the qualified because they've got that something inside them. And, you know, and all the qualifications in the world, I don't think necessarily make you have that affinity to children.

'Affinity to children' captures the tacit knowledge of early years practitioners, and interviewees particularly noted that it is typically mature practitioners, often those with parenting experience, who demonstrate that natural warmth and empathy. The annual increases in the National Minimum Wage for younger employees in the UK will hopefully deter some early years providers from trying to cut costs by deliberately recruiting younger staff on lower salaries. The introduction of an experience-based route into employment is, however, deeply concerning, as some providers may use this as an alternative to supporting employees to gain a full qualification.

Some differences between practitioners do not relate necessarily to age or qualification. Jordan, an Acorn manager, asserted: 'I don't think qualifications necessarily matter. You know, obviously, it comes down to, like, two types of people'; she then described her deputy, who was doing a degree, but not enjoying it, and had admitted she didn't think it would change her practice – it was just something she felt she ought to do; in contrast, Jordan described another colleague who is

> constantly trying to evolve. And I think the practitioners that are reflective and recognise that early years evolves constantly, and we

have to be adaptive, they're the people that, you know, that lead the nursery and that lead practice. And then you have the other people that are like, oh, I did my NNEB [National Nursery Examination Board qualification] and this is how we used to do it and, you know, the dinosaurs ... But how many times have we hired somebody straight from uni that, that doesn't know how to speak to a child ... you learn on the job, don't you?

Emily, a deputy manager at Acorn, having completed her degree several years after her initial qualification and after having had children, felt that doing this as a mature student 'makes it better because you've got the experience and you can relate it to the work that you're doing'. She described herself as a hands-on person who learns best through doing. The benefit of qualifications in terms of helping practitioners to be more reflective was described by Amber, an Acorn senior practitioner who was working towards a degree; she said: 'it made me look at my practice differently'.

Although a study by Mathers et al found a positive correlation between graduate leaders in early years settings and the quality of early education, 'staff experience and adult-child ratios were identified as being important for the more nurturing and "care-based" aspects of provision' (2011, p 4). This was a common theme in interviewees' responses, with several enthusing about fellow practitioners who have no qualifications but, as trainer and consultant Liz put it, 'might be better than the qualified because they've got that something inside them'. Those practitioners need to be given professional development opportunities, and more widely, a workforce development strategy that provides opportunities for all those working in early years would demonstrate a respect and care for early years professionals that is badly needed to address the ongoing difficulties in recruitment, retention and staff morale. Increasing the expectation that early years practitioners will have higher qualifications would undoubtedly have a positive impact on quality, and this would also have a positive impact on the perception of the profession as a valued career. This would also require improved pay scales, as well as better availability of funded training opportunities.

What the UK can learn from other countries

A recent comparison of early childhood systems in the Anglosphere (Moss and Mitchell, 2024) identified three distinctive features shared by the countries covered in the book: Australia, New Zealand, Canada, the US and three nations of the UK (Wales was not included). These shared characteristics are: first, systems which cover childcare for working families and/or early education; second, marketisation and privatisation; and, third, inadequate parenting leave. I discussed in Chapter 1 my disagreement with the call to 'ditch' childcare as a term and focus purely on early education, but I share Moss and Mitchell's concerns about marketisation and privatisation, and applaud their advocacy for improved parental leave. The adoption in the Anglosphere and France of a 'readiness for school' approach, in contrast to the tradition of social pedagogy in the Nordic and Central European countries, was noted by the OECD in 2006; the latter see the kindergarten as 'a broad preparation for life and the foundation stage of lifelong learning. The focus is placed on supporting children in their current developmental tasks and interests. The approach to children encompasses care, upbringing and education.' (OECD, 2006, p 57) This holistic approach is being threatened by an increased emphasis on accountability and measurable outcomes.

In 2016, on a study tour of Icelandic kindergartens, I was struck by the very different attitude to supervision and risk, particularly outdoors. Observing children climbing tall trees and a small toddler being pulled and pushed up onto a climbing frame by slightly older children in order to descend on one of the older child's laps, I reflected on how unlikely such scenes would be in the UK without an adult intervening or advising caution. When I pointed out the toddler's situation to one of the pedagogues, she breezily informed me that one of the older children was the toddler's sister, in a tone which implied that she therefore had full confidence in the sibling's care of her younger brother. There was similarly a confidence in the children's ability to manage their risks in tree climbing, with the focus of adult support being purely practical and tactical. From my initial concern that children seemed to be unsupervised, I soon realised that there was careful observation underway and subtle encouragement for children to navigate relationships and peer interactions without adult intervention.

A study of children's experiences in Icelandic preschools confirms this impression, with the children reflecting more on their friendships with other children than on the adults present, though when asked when they felt safe, 'they answered that they felt safe when they were close to the pedagogues' (Einarsdottir, 2017, p 67). The emphasis on 'care, social issues, play and child-initiated activities' (Einarsdottir, 2017, p 69), however, is under threat from a drive for more accountability, a heavier focus on academic achievement and a shortage of qualified play school teachers. In Iceland, teachers have postgraduate qualifications, but research there has shown that when qualified pedagogues are in the minority, they experience professional isolation and lack opportunities to share reflections and engage in discussion, confirming my impression of the positive impact of support for graduates through the Graduate Leader Fund, and the negative impact of the withdrawal of it a few years later (Mathers et al, 2011). The Icelandic curriculum places a much greater emphasis, compared to the UK, on care as an important value for children's learning and development, reflecting the social pedagogy approach of the Nordic countries.

Learning from other countries can include what not to do as well as learning from best practice examples. A book about the childcare crisis in America (Wuori, 2024) identifies its root cause as being a fundamental lack of understanding of the needs of young children and highlights the crucial importance of early education. Wuori (2024) details a series of public policy pitfalls which are not limited to the US, although some are exacerbated by the country's astonishing absence of paid parenting leave and lack of any national entitlement to ECCE services. Funding in the US is administered at a state level, but it is well below the OECD average (Moss and Mitchell, 2024). Wuori (2024, p 73) unpicks the unintended consequences of government funding policy which relies on market rate surveys and the requirement on states to set subsidy rates at only 75 per cent of average fee rates,

> leaving low-income parents limited to the very cheapest (and often worst) providers in the market and/or leaving providers in the position of accepting far less than their going rates to serve low-income children (a practice that results in the refusal of many top providers to participate in state subsidy systems at all).

Wuori (2024) lists seven pitfalls, or 'how not to solve the child care crisis', all of which have parallels with the situation in England. First, the over-reliance on publicly funded schools, rather than acknowledging the role of private, voluntary and independent providers, is an issue that is particularly resonant in the UK early years policy initiative of encouraging schools to expand into the nursery age range. As Wuori points out, schools are less likely to take on costly babies and toddlers, and focus instead on the preschool age range, where the staff-to-child ratio is higher and, therefore, more affordable. Without the preschool age groups, many private and voluntary providers would struggle to be financially sustainable. The second pitfall is the creation of demand without supply, which is exactly the effect of the extension of the funding entitlement in England when the number of early years providers is diminishing due to the problems of financial sustainability. The third pitfall is that funding rates are below the cost of delivery, and this is clearly a common feature in both the US and the UK. The fourth pitfall is basing funding on attendance (when costs don't diminish when a child is absent), which is a condition applied in some English local authorities, but not all. It's a pity that Wuori's book wasn't published in time for the UK government to take note of the fifth pitfall – thinking that diluting staff-to-child ratios will solve the affordability issue. In Wuori's words, 'loosening ratios and group size is not the way (to stabilise the sector). Even from a fiscal standpoint, it is – at best – tinkering around the edges in place of real reform. Don't fall into this trap' (2024, p 78). Wuori's sixth pitfall, 'relying on private equity to fill the void' (2024, p 78), is also highly relevant to the heavily marketised UK early years sector. As a Nuffield-funded University College London report concludes in relation to the situation in the UK, private for-profits tend to be dominated by highly leveraged financial models, and borrowing for company growth has not contributed to a growth of places for children (Simon et al, 2022). Wuori (2024) also notes the negative impact of the growth of the large nursery chains on smaller early years providers and the cost of provision for families. His final pitfall warns that relying on employers to provide on-site childcare, or funding for it, is not helpful for families not employed by large businesses, and one of the key messages of his book is that high-quality early years provision needs to be seen as a public good.

A comparison can also be made between the UK and Ireland, a country closer to home. There, a reform of the funding system appears to be improving the financial viability of the early years sector, increasing the amount of subsidy being received by families and improving the pay and qualification levels of the workforce. One notable difference is that the change process in Ireland 'has been and continues to be a genuine deliberative and forward-looking process, involving in-depth discussions and consultations with a wide range of stakeholders' (Lloyd, 2023, p 14). The new system combines increased funding with a combination of both supply-side and per-capita financing, and includes a legal underpinning for improvements to the early years workforce terms and conditions of employment. The increased policy attention to inclusion and to child and family poverty also distinguishes the model from the piecemeal gestures of the UK funding system, but at the time of writing it is still early days, and it remains to be seen whether the model adapts to rising costs effectively. Government policies, then, while they may be well-intentioned, rarely demonstrate an ethic of care or a real understanding of the issues facing the early years sector. Care involves attentive listening, and there is little evidence that those working in the sector have had their voice heard.

3

Can an organisation care?

Caring for the carers

Many organisations express a caring ethos in their policies and public statements, but in too many cases the protestations fail to translate into genuine care in practice and can better be described as 'carewashing' (Chatzidakis et al, 2020, p 11) or 'moral marketing gloss' (Puig de la Bellacasa, 2017, p 9). Whether there is a genuine intent to care is not the only issue here. Whether it is even possible for an organisation to care is also debatable (Kahn, 1993; Lawrence and Maitlis, 2012), with many endorsing Noddings' view that institutions cannot 'care for' in the sense prescribed by the ethics of care, but they can 'provide and support the conditions under which caring relations can prosper' (Noddings, 2015, p 83). Noddings advocates an approach based on the ideal of family life, as does Jane Roland Martin in her idea of a 'schoolhome' model for education (Martin, 1992; Noddings, 2002). Others focus more on the political perspective of power relations and the problems of reconciling care with organisational bureaucracy.

Care has been described as 'an organisational competence, a situated knowing that a group of professionals enact while attending to their everyday tasks' (Gherardi and Rodeschini, 2016, p 266). This practice-based approach to understanding caring is very relevant for the teamwork that takes place within nurseries, as attentive caring practice in early years is never entirely dependent on individuals, but often relies on collective competence and a shared orientation to care. Early years professionals are reliant on interdependent organisational practices and situated decision-making that has the interests of children as the priority. A collective, organisational ethic of care will inevitably facilitate care-full practices, but the ethic needs to be shared by those determining staffing levels and resources, not just those directly involved in delivering early years care and education; the issue is always whether caring rhetoric is matched with an understanding of what is needed to deliver high-quality care and the ability to resource it.

Caring for those who are themselves caregivers is clearly a key task for organisations which claim to be caring, yet the early years workforce is at risk of exploitation. The concept of emotional labour (Hochschild, 2012) has helped to highlight the potentially exploitative relationship between employers and employees, and that the need for those providing childcare to be emotionally accessible to the children they care for can lead to a risk of burn-out and emotional withdrawal if they are not themselves given emotional support. Staffing levels may often be limited to the minimum necessary for compliance, due to financial constraints, staff absences or recruitment difficulties, and situations will inevitably arise when individual children are in need of more one-to-one attention than the ratios allow. How supportive a management team is in those situations is one indication of how caring the culture of the organisation is. A nursery manager who gets stuck in to provide hands-on support to struggling colleagues is providing essential role-modelling – not just of practice, but of a caring culture.

I begin this chapter by focusing on how organisations care for their workforce because there is a direct relationship between the well-being of early years professionals and the quality of the care they provide to children and their families. When I asked interviewees about the ethical stance of early years organisations, I was struck by the number of comments about care, or lack of care, towards employees. These comments ranged from accounts of blatantly unethical practices exploiting the goodwill and vocational commitment of early years professionals to accounts of genuinely caring acts by individuals and different levels of support and trust. I was horrified at the account of Rachael, a nursery assistant, who was knocked unconscious briefly by a falling wooden parasol and was then given an ice pack and told to finish her shift. On going to the hospital after work, she discovered that she had fractured her shoulder and damaged the ligaments, but despite then being told by a physiotherapist to wear a sling, she reported: 'I was told I was not allowed to wear my sling at work because it would look bad to the parents.' She described feeling worthless and panicky whenever she had to speak to the manager, and said that she only stayed there after the incident because she was financially dependent on the job.

Less extreme, but equally uncaring and exploitative, is an account from Kim, a nursery manager, who described a situation early in her career when she worked for a private owner-manager. Despite being relatively newly qualified, she was often left to run the nursery:

> I worked seven o'clock to seven o'clock most days, and she was … quite emotionally manipulative in that because she lived there, if there were things left over to do, she would be like, 'oh, I've got to go and sort out my daughter' … and it was sort of like, 'will you stay and do the kitchen?' And I would, because I was very naive and easily persuaded at the time … she often would sit in the office and … I'd walk through and she was looking at Christmas shopping … she wasn't really involved, and a lot of it was left to me running it day to day.

Fortunately, I also heard many accounts of supportive, trusting and mutually respectful relationships with leaders and managers, and feelings of being valued at an organisational level. In fact, the most common complaint of 'they don't care' was voiced in relation to the government, particularly during the period during and after the COVID-19 pandemic. The lack of care described in those instances was often linked to the sector as a whole feeling undervalued. Schools and health professionals were often mentioned in government statements during the pandemic, but early years settings were only mentioned in passing, if at all, and with no thought or consideration for the fact that nurseries were staying open to care for the children of key workers and those deemed vulnerable. Social distancing and mask wearing are not possible with very small children, yet no recognition of that was made by those in government at the time, leaving early years professionals feeling uncared for. Organisationally, however, I heard accounts of careful, caring management during the crisis, as well as of caring environments being created – an aspect I explore further in Chapter 6. Childcare professionals need to be supported in their challenging roles if they are to be emotionally and physically present for the children they care for.

How organisations frame their purpose affects the priorities of those working in them. If the focus is on children, there needs to be a recognition of the importance of caring for those responsible for nurturing those children. As discussed in the previous chapter, recognising early years practitioners as professionals helps to facilitate a learning culture and a focus on high-quality provision, but at every level in the organisation, care needs to be embedded in policies and practice. This is particularly true within the management of people. In the Gallup Workforce Audit, the statement 'My supervisor or someone at work seems to care about me as a person' is identified as an important indicator of employee satisfaction and engagement (Harter et al, 2003). Feeling cared for may be interpreted in different ways by different people, but a sense of caring can help to bond individuals, and whether or not people feel cared for makes a difference to whether they deem their workplace to be part of a caring organisation. Employees who feel cared for are far more likely to make a discretionary contribution above and beyond their paid responsibilities, and a caring organisation will appreciate, not abuse, that goodwill.

The problem with profit as a key performance indicator

My interviews with a range of nursery managers demonstrated the influence that some corporate key performance indicators (KPIs) have on how success is measured in many early years organisations. I experienced this myself when asked to be a judge for a sector award of Nursery Manager of the Year. Some of the candidates from large nursery chains cited profitability statistics in their interviews, and one even brought a printed document as evidence of the financial success of her nursery. One manager interviewed in my research described a previous nursery as 'very corporate, all about FTEs [full-time equivalent places], marketing, meeting targets ... not really about the child' while another described her experience working in a similar role in a large nursery chain as 'very much like, these are your deadlines, these are the reports that need to be in on a Friday. You know, we don't really care about anything else kind of thing.'

Worryingly, several managers commented on their organisation's insistence on occupancy targets at the expense of anything else, with one, Helen, saying that she was told to 'never turn down a full-time place, even if you've got 18 children booked in for September for your nine-place baby room'. She said:

> It was all education ... I think because there was no care, their approach to staffing was different [to her current nursery]. And that showed in their horrendous staff turnover. It was not a nice place to be for the children because people were stressed, because it was always 'this room's got to be full, this business plan needs to be implemented'. It was never 'are the children happy?'

Tara, a manager at Acorn, described working at [a chain nursery]: 'it was just a pound sign. You would be overrun with children because they just wanted the room full for the money. They weren't interested in the stress, the pressure, the quality, anything for the children.' Similarly, Jordan, another Acorn manager, said: 'the bigger companies ... need to stand by those margins, don't they, because otherwise, you know, their shareholders are going to lose ... so, like the bigger it gets, the more there is on the line'.

One interviewee, Lucy, was a director of a group of nurseries, but had been a nursery manager in several organisations, and she contrasted the approaches of two very different nursery groups. In the first of these, she noted approvingly that the education team were 'very much part of everything', whereas in the second, she felt that the senior team 'were the most removed of any senior teams I've worked in ... it was almost like a completely separate function ... a very different culture'. In the second organisation, she felt that quality was 'a box-ticking exercise' with insufficient resources, so meaningful changes, that would have required working in partnership with those setting the budgets were impossible to implement. The awareness of profit as a KPI was also shown in interviews with nursery practitioners, who often commented on whether a nursery was 'all about money' or 'all about the children'.

The impact of the need for managers to increase their setting's profitability, where this is a primary business focus, is noted by Ofsted in their report on providers that operate multiple settings: 'nursery managers feel their multiple provider's ethos and values play out in their policies and working conditions' (Ofsted, 2021). My interviews confirmed that espoused values were not always followed through in practice, particularly in terms of a lack of autonomy for managers in decision-making over the allocation of funded places, and the same Ofsted report confirms this: 'where multiple providers suggest that they allow nursery managers to make the decision on the ratio of funded to unfunded places, this is not always the reality. Not all nursery managers feel that they are able or allowed to make this decision for their nursery.' The report also notes that for-profit providers often set profit margins for nursery managers to achieve, and these are monitored closely, with registered charities having 'different profit margin expectations for different nurseries depending on the demographics of the children in the nurseries'.

Being not-for-profit is not, however, a guarantee of ethical practice. An Acorn manger, Emily, explained that a nursery where she had worked previously operated as part of a larger charity, but it was run in a way which maximised profit, which was then diverted to the organisation's wider social purpose of tackling homelessness. 'The resources weren't fantastic … money didn't really come back into ourselves. It kind of got put into the homeless shelters … so we basically made a lot of money and it got put into different areas, not back into the nursery.' An organisation with an ethic of care would see profitability as a means to an end, rather than an end in itself. The difference is whether profit is being generated in order to increase returns for shareholders or to be reinvested into the organisation to improve resources, training, salaries as well as ensuring the continual improvement of quality and inclusivity. An organisation with social purpose, such as a social enterprise, would be mandated to do the latter.

Social enterprise and the ethics of care

Social entrepreneurs have been described as caring entrepreneurs who engage in entrepreneurial activities with the goal of fulfilling a social mission (André and Pache, 2016). Tronto's four phases of the ethics of care, discussed in more detail in the next chapter, can be applied to the entrepreneurial process, as seen in Table 3.1.

Bureaucracy may be seen as antithetical to entrepreneurship, and the term is usually used in a disparaging way. It has been rejected by some as a masculinist hierarchy of power (Ferguson, 1984) and antithetical to caring values (Bowden, 2000), but others have identified elements of bureaucracy that help to provide good governance (du Gay, 2000). It is often associated with larger organisations, particularly those in the public sector, and size can be a significant factor in determining how bureaucratic an organisation might become. Communication between owners, managers and staff teams can often be easier when nurseries are smaller or part of smaller groups. Larger

Table 3.1: Applying a care ethics framework to the entrepreneurial process

Entrepreneurial process	Social entrepreneurship process (care ethics framework)	Ethical practice implications for childcare organisations
Opportunity recognition: identifying needs/market gap	**'Caring about':** identifying the needs of others, particularly people in need – an 'engrossment' and empathic connection with others' situations	**Nursery locations:** identifying locations based on the childcare needs of local families; not targeting affluent areas or providing childcare that is unaffordable for many
Opportunity filtration: assessing the business case in terms of potential profitability	**'Taking care of':** deciding whether to act to meet the identified need based on a feeling of responsibility	**Policy decisions:** basing charging policies on criteria of affordability and accessibility (balanced with financial sustainability, rather than there being a focus on maximising profits)
Venture creation: developing the service	**'Care giving':** developing the provision of care as a service in a way which demonstrates a caring attitude	**Embedding care into practice:** ensuring that childcare practices are delivered with sensitivity and respect
Exchange stage: an iterative process of refining, adapting and improving the service, shaped by the exchange of information between entrepreneurs and stakeholders	**'Care receiving':** critically analysing how care is received and its impact by listening to care recipients' needs and their assessment of the care received	**Reflexive practice:** ensuring that childcare practitioners reflect on their practice, gain feedback from parents and other stakeholders, and evaluate the impact on the children, including capturing the children's voices

Source: After André and Pache (2016)

nurseries and larger chains, of necessity, need more formal communication channels, which can give an impersonal effect that is at odds with the relationality needed for an ethic of care.

Encouragingly, there appears to be a growing interest in, and awareness of, the impact of the ownership and governance arrangements of early years organisations, and moves are underway to raise the profile of early years social enterprises. A key recommendation of a 2024 report from the IPPR and Save the Children (Reed and O'Halloran, 2024) is to establish new not-for-profit nursery trusts, recognising that this might offer the best opportunity for nurturing high-quality provision for disadvantaged children. Maintained nursery schools offer high quality, but usually for a limited number of hours, plus they are few in number. Their costs are significantly higher compared to the private and voluntary sector, which is not a coincidence as they usually have more highly qualified and better-paid early years teachers. An

IPPR report from 2022 notes the need to limit profits for private settings to ensure funding is spent on improving provision and staff pay, but also observes that 'this would be extremely hard to do in practice, given the range of accountancy tricks that could be used to get around any cap' (Statham et al, 2022, p 26). Social enterprises, particularly those with charitable status, could provide a more transparent and socially focused financial model. It remains to be seen whether the 2024 report has any greater impact than the one from 2022. A more recent report on social enterprises in the early years sector (Reed, 2025) raises the profile of this potential. And for the first time, the government strategy for the sector has specific mentions of social enterprises having a role to play (Department for Education, 2025c).

Ethical slippage and the unintended consequences of non-caring and acaring policies

In my research interviews, several examples of unethical practice were described, sometimes in response to questions about what constitutes ethical practice. For example, interviewees often commented that 'it's easier to describe what *isn't* ethical practice'. The everyday nature of care, as Peta Bowden (1997) observes, can produce an 'aura of invisibility', and care is often taken for granted, only being noted when it fails or falls short. Whether a lack of care is noticeable also depends on the culture and habitual behaviours within a setting. In a nursery where practitioners are expected to respond promptly and sympathetically to any signs of distress, a crying child will evoke concern and a call for action. If a nursery or a group of practitioners within a nursery adopts the expectation that children need to learn not to expect responsiveness immediately, the sound of crying may not trigger a similar reaction, and the phrase 'you're alright, don't cry' may be heard. An absence of care such as this would be non-caring, to adopt Hamington's categories: in addition to 'caring' and 'noncaring', he identifies a third category of 'acaring', which describes a morally neutral pattern or habit (Hamington, 2004). In not consciously adopting a caring intent, policies that appear to be neutral, or acaring, can in fact lead to a damaging absence of care.

Ethical slippage can arise from a lack of empathy and an unquestioning acceptance of policies that have produced unintended consequences. One interviewee, for example, described how a child had to be prevented from seeing her sibling going from the adjacent room to the garden, as she would get upset and the older sibling would also then be upset at seeing his baby sister in tears. The commentary was purely about the practical logistics of keeping the siblings apart and out of sight of each other, and it was clearly not permissible to contemplate the idea of allowing some contact between them as an alternative way to avoid upset. Similarly, moving a child from one age group to another to achieve optimal efficiency in terms of ratios and occupancy was often given as an example of financial efficiency overriding the emotional well-being of the child, especially if that child was not ready for the transition or was being moved without any peers moving up at the same time, thereby losing continuity of friendships.

The policy of moving children up to the next age group immediately after their second birthday is an example of an acaring policy. There is nothing 'uncaring' about it, but the child's personal well-being and social and emotional development isn't being taken into account, so it is not a care-full decision, just an operationally efficient move. Most nurseries, I'm happy to report, take a more thoughtful approach to transitions and will usually move a cohort of children together and only after considering which children are ready for such a move, rather than relying purely on biological age. Only rarely do children keep their key person throughout their time at nursery, and the number of transitions a child experiences between age groups, each involving a new key person, is often exacerbated by changes of key person within the age group when there is turnover within the staff team. A decision to move staff between rooms, or between nurseries, needs to take into account how continuity of care for children can best be protected.

Ethical slippage can also begin with a simple lack of attentiveness to quality. Ros, a trainer and consultant, described an example of this with an owner who lacked an understanding of what constituted good practice:

> So I went into this beautiful nursery ... all the children were in different corners, so they must have been put into small groups after lunch ... and I watched them ... one member of staff was just sat there [mimes bored position, head resting on hand]. And, and I just thought, God, that's terrible. So I said this to [owner's name]. She said, 'Oh, I thought it all looked really like the children were all being well-behaved.' I said, 'Well, it might have looked that they're being well-behaved because they weren't doing anything. They weren't happy' ... And so they thought being quiet was well-behaved, not recognising that what was taking place was really mediocre.

On another occasion, Ros expressed frustration with practitioners' lack of recognition of the poor quality of care being provided at the end of a morning session:

> When some children went home and some went for lunch, it was [closes eyes and shakes her head] ... Nobody was doing anything. I said, 'Shouldn't one of you read a story or something?' And they were all sitting there and every so often a child would leave or somebody else would go and wash their hands. And after they'd all gone, I said, 'Can

you explain to me what was going on?' And they said, 'Oh, well, some of those children go home for lunch and some stay.' I said, 'Well ... I've been watching this poor little girl. She stayed longer than the others ... sitting there for ages watching all the other children going for lunch.'

The lack of care about that child's emotional well-being demonstrates a lack of attentiveness that can happen at a practice level within nurseries. However, the responsibility in both of the scenarios described here surely lies with the senior staff within the rooms or the nursery management team, who should be able to evaluate the quality of care and education being provided at all times of the day and pick up on those periods when nothing much is happening or when early years practitioners are disengaged or inattentive. The government's decision not to fund meals as part of the 'free entitlement' was also a factor in this scenario, with the nursery offering the option of collecting children just before lunchtime as their solution.

The leadership of an organisation may also affect the ability of a nursery to create a caring culture through the decisions they make about the initial design and set-up. In my interviews, asking about views on the ideal size of a nursery elicited a range of responses, and these tended to correlate with the role of the interviewee. Directors made comments like 'the bigger the setting the better' or 'there's no point doing one less than 75, 80', with 126 being cited as an optimum size. Conversely, nursery managers tended not to share the desire for larger sites. Sinead, a Level 3 manager in a large chain of nurseries, felt that the size of her nursery, with 64 places, is

> perfect, our room sizes are perfect, you know, you have so many children that you can supervise, look after, and provide that care and well-being ... funnily enough we have got an application for a loft conversion. As much as I'm like, yeah, because we've got the demand, you know, the demand is there, but part of me's like [sucks her teeth]. And to put an upstairs, you don't want to segregate people then either.

Similarly Caroline, an owner-manager with a Montessori qualification, expressed a preference for the size of her nursery, with 36 places, saying that she worried about the impact on quality with larger nurseries: 'I don't think that you can have the same quality control when you have 20 members of staff coming and going ... I don't think I'd want to get a lot bigger. I don't, I would rather have a second small nursery ... than make this any bigger.' She also commented on it being easier for her nursery to adapt the settling-in process to the needs of individual families, mentioning that staff members had also observed the difference compared to other settings: 'They've come from several chains and they've never seen that before, where an owner will work with the parents on settling-in sessions that work for the child and the parent.' Sam, a trustee of another small nursery, explained that the size of the nursery was limited by the size of the building and commented that 'if it was a commercial nursery using that space, probably they would build into quite a lot of the garden space because that would allow them to carry more kids', while for them the green space was particularly important, as they were situated in a city where 'lots of the parents who are living locally are in flats so they don't have immediate access to outside space'.

The question of first (or even second) floors in nurseries is an ethical issue that is rarely discussed, but this came up in several of my research interviews and is something I have personally considered to be a significant influence on quality of provision, particularly in determining the ease of access to outdoor play areas. Sinead's reluctance for her nursery to expand upwards, mentioned earlier, was echoed by others' comments about very large nurseries over more than one floor. I also visited a nursery within a large group that had one upstairs room; this was used to house funded-only children, who were segregated from the part-funded places. The area manager who showed me around described the room as being a practical solution to ensure the shorter funded-only sessions didn't disrupt those children who were attending for longer days. But it was also clear that only the children downstairs had meals included and a full range of activities. Also, the room upstairs was the only one without direct access to the outdoors. The team seemed oblivious to the two-tier nature of provision being offered.

Similarly, trainer and consultant Ros described overhearing company directors saying: 'Oh, we'll buy that site. Yeah, there's no garden, but we'll make the staff go around the corner to the park.' She commented: 'I'm sitting there thinking from a quality perspective, and an ethical perspective, that's not the right way to be looking at it.' Ros had been taken on by the company to address issues of quality, but this was only covered at the end of each meeting. She noted that there was a 'lack of recognition that the core business was about children. I went to one meeting and somebody fed back afterwards and said: "You were the only person that mentioned children in that entire meeting."' The attitude Ros described, of focusing purely on the commercial aspect of operating nurseries, is perhaps not deliberately 'uncaring', but rather an example of 'acaring' in that the needs of young children are not taken into account.

When nurseries have playrooms on upper floors, these are often used for the very youngest children – a decision which has been questioned (Norman, 2019), but which reflects the greater likelihood of older children to make more use of free-flow opportunities to outdoor areas. There are other concerns to be taken into account, including the impact on evacuation procedures. Although in an ideal world, all nurseries would have all their playrooms on the ground floor, this is unrealistic in many towns and cities. However, choosing to open a nursery in a building with no outdoor play area severely limits the opportunities for children to participate in outdoor play activities, as supervised visits to local parks cannot offer the same play experiences as a nursery garden with an area for growing fruit and vegetables, a sandpit and water tray, a mud kitchen and a room for wheeled toys, games and den building.

Leadership and culture

The leadership of an organisation is a critical factor in determining how ethical the childcare provision is and a major influence on the culture of early years provision. There was consensus among my interviewees that the culture, ethos and values of a nursery are strongly influenced, if not created, by those at the top. Two of the leaders I interviewed were consistently praised by interviewees who worked, or had worked, at nurseries in their organisations. Peter insisted that his company's success was all down to the people within it, and John described maintaining 'a moral compass' as one of the most challenging but important aspects of his role. Both were similarly critical of government policy, but expressed different perceptions of care. Whereas Peter asserted that 'care drives the outcomes financially', John felt that 'care has been the downfall' in that it implies a private responsibility, which is in contrast to the nature of public funding for education.

The two statements address different aspects of the word 'care'. Peter recognised that the quality of care (of employees as well as of children) is the single biggest determinant of financial success, as that depends on parental and staff satisfaction, while John's words focused on the perception of childcare as a kind of babysitting service rather than it being seen as a profession. Both leaders were described by their employees as being genuinely interested in and concerned about their colleagues and as leading by example. In contrast, other interviewees described leaders who would complain vociferously about the inadequacies of government funding, but 'then turn around and say "Oh, I'm off to the Bahamas for six weeks."' There were also comments about leaders who made no secret of the profitability of a nursery being their primary concern, including cutting corners wherever possible.

Policies, decisions and interpretations of official guidance are usually determined by the management team at a nursery, although the degree to which leadership is distributed among a wider cohort varies widely. The role of nursery manager is also subject to a variety of interpretations and expectations. Smaller nurseries are likely to need a manager who is happy to be hands-on with the children on a regular basis, but larger nurseries often have managers who are office based and rarely engage in practice within the rooms. One of my interviewees, when she was a manager at a large corporate chain, had been instructed to take the latter approach, but found it very frustrating.

> I was told never to be in the room. I was told I that I had a deputy who I could send in and she could report back to me, which is spying. I had CCTV that I was encouraged to use. And I was told that my place was to balance budgets.

She left that setting 'because it was KPIs, it was business plans', rather than being focused on the children. The size of an organisation is not necessarily the critical factor in determining the level of autonomy of a manager, as some interviewees described private owners of single nurseries or small groups as being very dictatorial about nursery policies and practice. Sinead described a climate of fear emanating from her previous nursery owner: 'it was [owner]'s way or no way ... you had to conform. And, you know, you heard stories if you didn't, you knew what would happen.'

Organisational culture, often described as 'the way we do things around here', is another important influence on practice. With many practitioners now undertaking their vocational training 'on the job' as apprentices, the community of practice within a nursery is hugely influential on the caring habits of practitioners in training. But culture is also about the emotional atmosphere of a setting. Maria, a nursery parent, reflected on the importance of the general 'feel' of a nursery and made a direct comparison with her hospital workplace:

> It's a bit like, for me, it's a bit like in nursing ... no matter who comes on that ward, it's about the, the feeling on that ward. And it does come down to the individual, [their] group, and it comes down to the leadership as well, about how it makes you feel. The hundred steps when you come onto a ward, you can tell how that ward is going to run by just walking on and getting that feel about it.

The differences between leadership and management are often debated, and leadership is often viewed as a quality rather than as a role. In one example of leadership from my research interviews, Tara gave an account of being a new manager at a nursery and having to intervene in a mealtime routine. A new baby, who was still settling in, was in a high chair but was clearly very distressed and not eating anything. Tara told the early years practitioner who was with the child to take him out of the highchair, comfort him and then, if necessary, feed him on her lap. 'Are we allowed to do that?' was the response, as the practitioner clearly felt that the 'rule' was to feed babies only when they were in highchairs. Tara's response was to explain that 'you do whatever's right for the child. If that child's sitting in the highchair crying because he's really scared and he doesn't know anybody, you need to sit him on your lap, get him used to you ... feed him sitting on your lap. It's small steps.' In this example, the normal mealtime policy was overridden by Tara's determination to create a more caring culture, which meant empowering practitioners to adapt daily routines to fit the individual needs of the children. Culture is the 'way we do things around here', and Tara embarked on a mission to change the rule-bound routines she found at the nursery with a more caring and responsive approach.

A study undertaken in a UK state school found that whereas the senior leadership team prioritised grades and fairness, classroom teachers put the emphasis on a broader social education, responding to students' individual needs (Edwards et al, 2023). The authors of the study contrasted these approaches as a justice-based and feminist ethic of care, respectively, and suggested that a 'parentalist' ethic of care might usefully combine both roles – not relying only on a gender-neutral style of parenting, but combining the feminist ethic of care with the traditionally 'masculine' ethic of justice. The association of the ethic of care with hands-on teachers while the ethic of justice is associated with management is, I suggest, more to do with the nature of the roles than gender. An ethic of care is inevitably more easily understood by those dealing with individual children than by those focusing on measurable outcomes. In a different study, comparing two types of early years settings, researchers found that 'settings that prioritised care and socialisation fostered an interactive micro-climate which was more favourable to co-construction than those which emphasised educational outcomes' (Georgeson, 2009, p 109). These two studies are not directly comparable, but they each identify approaches that reflect the leadership and culture of the settings and how these can have a direct impact on pedagogy. A relational pedagogy has a natural affinity with an ethic of care; both recognise the primacy of relationships and the interdependence and interconnectivity of children and adults. Relational pedagogy, therefore, offers an alternative approach to a focus on 'school-readiness' (Papatheodorou, 2009). Ultimately, the leadership and culture of a setting will determine the extent to which an ethic of care can be embedded, but adopting a relational pedagogy is a facilitating factor.

4

Care ethics in childcare practice

From feminine to relational – the development of care ethics

The ethics of care is rooted in maternalism, but this factor may also have contributed to the undervaluing of early years professionals. The term does not describe the relationship of a mother to her child, but 'the cultural understandings attributed to this role by society' (Ailwood, 2007, p 157). Maternalism has been associated with childcare for many years. The German inventor of kindergartens, Friedrich Froebel, saw maternalism as the basis for being a good early years practitioner, although his ideas were mocked at the time. His suggestion in 1844 that women should be able to train to teach children was greeted with laughter from his all-male audience (Bruce, 2021). Froebel's idea was that an early years teacher should operate as a 'mother made conscious' (Steedman, 1985) and that good teaching would be based on what good mothers did naturally, but making it more overt.

The conflation of mothering and teaching, or the idea of teaching as a version of mothering, can be seen as the feminisation of a trade, similar to perspectives on professions such as nursing and midwifery. In the early part of the 19th century, the majority of teachers of young children were men, and the recruitment of women into the teaching workforce was seen as way for working-class women to enter a profession and therefore improve their social standing. Carolyn Steedman (1985) argued that the feminine was then reified and formalised within the theory and practice of primary schooling, with an inevitable emphasis on care rather than education, a tension which has influenced early years education and care ever since.

Another influential figure in early years care and education was Maria Montessori. She was the first Italian woman to graduate with a medical degree, in 1896, and she based her ideas in scientific research. This undoubtedly helped her ideas to be accepted, particularly as she combined them with an idealisation of mothers and more traditional perceptions on the role of female teachers of young children, advising: 'She should study her movements, making them as gentle and graceful as possible, that the child may unconsciously pay her the compliment of thinking her as beautiful as his mother, who is naturally his ideal of beauty' (quoted in Ailwood, 2007, p 87). Both Montessori and Froebel were key figures of the kindergarten movement, which focused on love, care and maternalism to varying degrees but which also began the professionalisation of early care and education.

There is undoubtedly a tension between maternalism and professionalisation within the early years sector, and maternalism is arguably a contributory factor in the low pay of the early years workforce.

Sara Ruddick, a feminist philosopher, has been credited with beginning the discourse around ethics and care, and her concept of maternal thinking 'arises out of actual child-caring practices' (1980, p 346). Ruddick's argument was that the experience of mothering and maternal practices gives rise to a different way of thinking, in the tradition of Habermas, Wittgenstein and others who, she said, contend that '*all* thought arises out of social practice' (Ruddick, 1980, p 347, emphasis in original). Thinking, she argued, 'is governed by the interests of the practice out of which it arises, and the act of thinking names and elaborates the "given" reality to whose demands practice is responding' (Ruddick, 1980, p 347). Nearly thirty years later, Ruddick clarified that she had set out 'to elucidate the "*rationality* of *care*," taking mothering, and the maternal thinking it expresses, as a primary instance' (Ruddick, 2009, p 305, emphasis in original). She explained in the later essay that she rejected the idea of 'women's intuition' or 'feminine sensibility' as marking an absence of mind or thought, and in her 1989 book on maternal thinking, she expanded on her 'practicalist' view that 'thinking arises from and is tested against practices' (Ruddick, 1989, p 13). She consistently argued that intellectual activities cannot be separated from disciplines of feeling, describing maternal thinking as 'a unity of reflection, judgment and emotion' (Ruddick, 1980, p 348). This resonates with the under-appreciation of the underpinning complexity of early years work (Goldstein, 1998) and the recognition within the early years sector of the importance of reflection that acknowledges the emotional and affective aspects of early years practice (Osgood, 2010).

Ruddick also recognised the importance of embodied and sensory learning for children, pointing out that children do not 'distinguish in their bodily lives between rich elaborate mental play and the "merely physical"' (Ruddick, 1989, p 206). She identified three elements of maternal practice: preservation of the child, fostering growth and guiding people to be socially acceptable. These are not dissimilar to the priorities of most early childhood provision; keeping children safe from harm, nurturing their development and preparing them for life in today's society – 'socially acceptable' might also be seen as one way of describing 'school-readiness'. She was also clear that her idea of mothering was not dependent on a biological relationship, arguing that in an ideal world, there would be no more fathers, but 'mothers of both sexes' (Ruddick 1980, p 362) . This dismissal of fatherhood is dated, and Ruddick has also been criticised for ethnocentrism and universalising, but she was a trail-blazer in taking childcare practices seriously and in recognising both the complexity of thought involved in caring for the very youngest and the ethical dimension of care.

The landmark book by Carol Gilligan (1982) on the 'different voice' of women was probably even more influential than Ruddick's book, and her exploration of maternal consciousness is relevant for a workforce which is predominantly female and working in loco parentis. Gilligan was a psychologist, and her work was groundbreaking in challenging the rights and responsibilities view of morality and in arguing that girls and women approach ethical problems from a more relational perspective, which she viewed as a moral strength, not a weakness. In her insistence on women having a different voice, Gilligan could, like Ruddick, be accused of reinforcing gender stereotypes, but in later works Gilligan and Snider developed a persuasive argument recognising that the relational voice could help to combat patriarchy, the hierarchy of which, they argued, 'is premised on a loss of relationship and thereby on a sacrifice of love. Conversely, democracy, like love, is contingent on relationship' (2018, p 145).

Like Ruddick, Gilligan made it clear that her distinction between male and female voices was 'a distinction between two modes of thought ... rather than to represent a generalization about either sex' (1982, p 2). Some of her early generalisations about women's experiences and attitudes feel outdated, but in citing Piaget's influence on views of child development related to the need for greater care and respect of differences, she provided a rich seedbed for later child psychologists in terms of the importance of caring relations and connections (Zeedyk, 2006). Gilligan's main message was that women have an 'overriding concern with relationships and responsibilities' (1982, p 16), a theme which was taken up shortly after by Nel Noddings, who took the relational perspective a step further and undertook one of the most detailed and significant studies of ethical care practices.

The original subtitle of Noddings' most well-known book, *Caring* (published in 1984), was *A Feminine Approach to Ethics and Moral Education*. Nearly thirty years later, she changed this to *A Relational Approach to Ethics and Moral Education* (Noddings, 2013, p xiii), recognising, perhaps, that tying the approach to gender was potentially limiting and misleading, but also reflecting her growing belief in the importance of the caring relation. To begin with, Noddings, citing Gilligan, explained: 'I have called the language used in *Caring* the language of the mother, as contrasted with that of the father' (2013, p xiii); she further explained that she was keen not to lose 'the centrality of women's experience in care ethics' (2013, p xiii), later extending her argument about maternal instinct being a source of morality (Noddings, 2010b). She is probably best known for her phenomenological analysis of care and for her distinction between types of care and caring.

Noddings began *Caring* by asserting her belief that the caring relation is ethically basic, locating 'the very wellspring of ethical behavior in human affective response' (Noddings, 2013, p 3). In focusing on the motivation for caring, she then outlined her concept of 'natural' caring. This, according to Noddings, is 'the social condition we treasure and want to establish or preserve' (2013, p xv). She described maternal and other instinctive caring as being motivated by love or inclination. She argued that this commitment and self-definition of being the 'one-caring' is not just a manifestation of morality but the foundation of it, with a commitment to care guiding an 'ethical ideal'. Noddings contrasted the instinctive behaviour of many parents with a conscious decision to care, which she described as 'ethical caring', requiring a more deliberate intent. Noddings later explained that she did not 'mean to suggest that the capacity for natural caring does not need cultivation' (Noddings, 2002, p 29), but that the self-identification of ourselves as caring helps us to overcome a dislike or resentment of caring tasks and responsibilities. This is clearly relevant for those in paid caring roles, such as childcare roles, as is her argument that the act of caring for others helps to develop the moral orientation of an ethic of care and that if children can see and assist in genuine caring done by adults, this can act as an 'incubator for the development of caring' (Noddings, 2013, p xiv).

One aspect of Noddings' relational approach is the insistence on the importance of reciprocity from the 'cared-for'. Potentially there may be instances where children are unable to provide the response that Noddings considered to be crucial, particularly if they have developmental delays or cognitive impairment or if they are neurodivergent, but as with nonverbal babies and toddlers, carers can often ascertain a response by observing body language and facial expressions carefully, and proactively asking for feedback can often elicit a smile or grimace, giving an opportunity for reciprocal expressions. Noddings also made a useful differentiation between receptive, attentive caring and empathy. She engaged in a debate with Michael Slote, a professor of ethics, over his interpretation of the term empathy and argued that it 'retains a heavy cognitive connotation' (Noddings, 2010a, p 6). Noddings described a chain of events in a caring process as beginning with attentiveness to another's situation, which she insisted necessarily precedes empathy. When the 'one-caring' then puts aside their own personal goals or purposes in order to satisfy another's needs, Noddings called this 'motivational displacement', and the point of what she called 'ethical' rather than 'natural' caring is that this might require a deliberate decision to overcome personal reluctance. The focus on motivation for caring has, however, been criticised as a weakness (Fisher and Tronto, 1990) in that it suggests an assumption that with the right motivation, caring becomes unproblematic, disregarding issues of power relations, which I explore later in the chapter as this also applies to the potential exploitation of the early years workforce.

Table 4.1 summarises the ethics of care theorists most relevant to early years practice, indicating their key texts. These highlight the influence of maternalism, a range of disciplines that have developed the ethic of care, and the increased focus on its moral and political aspects, highlighting the role

Table 4.1: Ethics of care theorists

Author	Discipline	Key works and overview
Nancy Chodorow	Psychoanalytic sociology	*The Reproduction of Mothering* (1978) – argues that social construction of gender roles is created by males and females being mothered differently
Sara Ruddick	Philosophy	'Maternal thinking' (1980) – first to argue that different thinking practices emerge from childcaring practices; *Maternal Thinking* (1989) extends this argument to politics of peace
Carol Gilligan	Psychology and ethics	*In a Different Voice* (1982) – argues that women think differently to men, with their relational perspective creating an ethic of care (related to justice)
Nel Noddings	Philosophy and education	*Caring* (1984) – takes a relational and phenomenological approach to the ethic of care and applies it to education
Joan Tronto	Political science	*Moral Boundaries* (1993) – describes four phases of care and argues for a moral and political ethic of care
Peta Bowden	Philosophy (feminist ethics)	*Caring* (1997) – focuses on the complexity of caring practices rather than principles of caring
Maurice Hamington	Feminist philosophy and ethics	*Embodied Care* (2004) – argues that embodied practices of ethical care can provide a transformative approach to social justice
Virginia Held	Philosophy	*The Ethics of Care* (2006) – argues for care ethics to be used as a moral framework and for care to be seen as fundamental

of an ethic of care as being supportive of social justice, as well as deepening an understanding of the importance and nature of care:

'Mothers of both sexes': the gender issue

It has been argued that 'care ethics has ... tended to conflate sex and gender with the universalizing narrative of "motherhood" and has under-theorized the relation of care to power' (Cloyes, 2002, p 212). Care has been described as 'both an opportunity and a danger in relation to work with young children' (Barnes, 2019, p 17), recognising the ambivalent and sometimes negative connotations of the concept of care, particularly in the early years sector, in relation to education. Feminists are understandably wary of the oppressive potential of caring roles. Noddings' distinction between 'ethical' and 'natural' caring is useful for considering care ethics in relation to a paid workforce instead of familial, unpaid childcare, and interviewees in my study discussed the extent to which caring skills are natural, or innate, rather than deliberately cultivated. Ruddick contrasted the kinds of care given by a father taking his child to a day care centre and the day care worker caring for the child, describing the caring effort of the father as a response to his relationship with the child, whereas the caring effort of the day care worker is more likely to be in response to her work role (Ruddick, 1998).

The persistence of the 'full-time mothering ideological norm' was the result of women remaining almost universally in charge of the care of infants and young children for many generations (Chodorow, 2000, p 346; see also Chodorow, 1978). 'Fathering' still has very different connotations to 'mothering', but there is increasing recognition of the need for equally shared parental roles. One of the concerns raised by feminists in relation to the ethic of care has been that in asserting the need to base childcare practice on mothering, or familial care, there is a danger of perpetuating the exploitation of women in childcaring roles within the family. As Fine put it: 'The school drop-off is political, the staying home when the kids are sick is political' (2010, p 79).

Winnicott, a psychoanalyst and paediatrician, who is perhaps most famous for his concept of the 'good-enough mother', differentiated parental roles on gendered lines, describing the maternal role as child focused and caring, while the paternal role is protective and externally facing (Winnicott, 1971). It is now widely recognised that the gendering of parental roles is the product of social engineering and not biology, and that men, women and non-binary individuals may take on all aspects of parenting and caring roles equally. Care ethics and the historic, but pervasive, view of care being a feminine attribute are often conflated with feminist and feminine ethics. Compassion, empathy and kindness are often seen as feminine traits, and this emphasises the need to recognise care ethics as relational, personal, and gender-neutral. Improving the gender balance of the early years workforce would help to change archaic gendered perceptions of care, and there also needs to be an awareness of the risk of perpetuating gender stereotypes if male staff in early years settings are encouraged to take on the outdoor, active roles in preference to spending time in caring practices. Winnicott's differentiation of parental roles may sound outdated to many of us, but we still have a long way to go to change the mindset of many people in wider society, and we must recognise that care, including childcare, continues to be gendered.

The COVID-19 pandemic proved this point. Mothers disproportionately took on childcare responsibilities during the period when childcare settings were closed to the majority of families (Sevilla and Smith, 2020), and early years professionals, mostly women, who continued to work (as many nurseries remained open for keyworker families and vulnerable children) received very little recognition, whether in the UK (Early Years Alliance, 2021; Hardy et al, 2022) or in other countries, such as Canada (Richardson et al, 2021). My post-pandemic interviewees echoed these findings, with several mentioning the low morale that resulted from the absence of any mention of nurseries in the regular government announcements and public expressions of thanks to health professionals.

Gender can also give rise to ethical dilemmas for practitioners when parents make requests based on personal beliefs and concerns that do not sit comfortably with a nursery's ethos of inclusive practice. Cara, for example, narrated an exchange with a parent who had heard that 'Clive' was going to be their daughter's key person. The parent said:

> 'That's really good. But he won't change her nappy, will he?' 'Well, yeah, because he's her key worker.' 'Oh, but he's a bloke.' 'Yeah.' So I said, 'What is it … that's worrying you about that?' And he said, 'Well, you know, he's a man, he shouldn't be changing my daughter's nappy.' 'Oh, so do you not change your daughter's nappy, then, as a man?' 'Well I do, but I'm her dad.' So, so we had to do quite a lot of work with that family, who ended up being Clive's biggest fan.

Cara came across in her interview as a skilful, confident communicator, so it was perhaps not surprising that she reached a successful resolution with that family. It probably also helped that Clive was a mature practitioner with a family of his own. In another example, in one of our own nurseries, a family removed their child on hearing that a male practitioner had been appointed, without even meeting him. My interviews and wider research data confirmed my own perceptions of ongoing gender prejudice.

The persistence of such prejudice against men in early years settings is perhaps one reason why the numerous initiatives to recruit more men into the childcare workforce have made very slow progress. As is clear from the ongoing work of the organisation Let Toys Be Toys, the perpetuation of stereotypical roles for children in children's clothing and toys is still ongoing. The early years sector has had a long-standing commitment to gender-neutrality (Peeters, 2013), but as several neuroscientists have shown, the prevalence of unconscious bias is much harder to tackle, both with the general public and with the early years workforce (Fine, 2010; 2017; Saini, 2017; Rippon, 2019). The sector's reputation for low pay is probably also a factor in the struggle to recruit men, as illustrated by graduate manager Jordan's wry comment: 'Why haven't we got more men in early years? Because of the stigma? Because of the money, probably.'

On one occasion, when I was showing a local Member of Parliament round one of our nurseries, as well as bending his ear about the issue of making meals 'optional extras', I mentioned the difficulties of attracting men to work in early years provision. On introducing him to Alan, one of our male practitioners, he asked him why he thought more men weren't choosing early years careers, and Alan's response was to ask him whether he ever considered it himself. Our Member of Parliament looked slightly taken aback and acknowledged that when he was at school, it wasn't ever suggested as an option, except for girls. Hopefully that is changing, but there is a long way to go to achieve a gender-balanced workforce.

Ethics of care and early years practice

The relevance of the ethics of care for early years practice is increasingly recognised (Goldstein, 1998; Langford, 2019; Rosen, 2019; Taggart, 2019). The reason for this is threefold. First, the focus on the role of women as primary carers addresses an ongoing feminist challenge, which is still very relevant in a sector where 98 per cent of the workforce is female (Bonetti, 2019). Despite an increasing acknowledgement in many societies that childcare is an issue for working families, not just for mothers, women still shoulder a disproportionate amount of childcaring responsibilities. The ethics of care recognises the relation of power and care, both in the allocation of responsibility and in the implementation of care practices. Second, the phenomenological focus on the relationality of care practices is particularly helpful in the analysis of embodied, tacit knowledge and skills (Hamington, 2004). Third, the ethics of care recognises both the vital importance of care within educational settings and the ways in which the concept of care spans levels of analysis, from macro to micro, from the political, social and organisational down to individual relationships and acts of caring practice. As Seigfried (1996, p 207) put it 'there is something about caring that ought to be central to value systems'.

Children need to feel loved in order to be able to learn and develop effectively, (Gerhardt, 2004), and there is increased recognition of the need for 'care, concern and connection' (Martin, 1992, p 34), care as an attitude (Noddings, 2002) and care as a moral practice (Tronto, 1993). Sometimes, however, care is seen as a buzzword in education, neglecting the complexity underlying the nature of the work involved (Goldstein, 1998). A care perspective as a moral theory can have global relevance, with early years settings playing a role in the social and emotional development of future generations. Caring can be 'transformative' for children, and, it can be argued, feminist moral theory can be seen to 'develop around the priority of the flourishing of children in favourable environments' (Held, 1993, p 87). Apart from the importance of nurturing care and education for young children, the ethic of care, as a feminist moral theory, takes account of the needs of working mothers and challenges the exploitation of the poorly paid, undervalued, largely female workforce in the sector. Moral issues are frequently encountered in childcare practice, and the relational approach of an ethic of care is the most appropriate perspective for examining the influences that make a difference in the care of children, for the children, their parents, the practitioners in the settings and, more widely, society.

Embedding an ethic of care into practice in early years settings involves embedding care-full practice with the children, which is characterised by respectful, attentive and thoughtful interactions at a pace which fits the needs of children. It also means that care as an ethic needs to be applied to the whole staff team, the families of the children attending, the local community and the natural environment. Caring is a universal human activity, and in the world of early years, adults are role models for the next generation, so we need to be seen to be caring for objects, plants, animals and ourselves. Children imitate what they experience, and instilling an ethic of care across the organisation is good early years practice as well as being beneficial to all. It is not as simple as simply caring in a kind and gentle way. Caring leadership, which is critical for early years settings, 'has little to do with compassion, kindness or niceness; it involves and requires a fundamental organization and leadership of self' (Tomkins and Simpson, 2015, p 1013). An ethic of care focuses on moral development and a wider consideration of care as an organisational practice. Good early years practice is naturally caring, so it is a process of extending that ethic of care into all aspects of an organisation's work. It is an enactment of care in ways that deliberately empower and enable others and in ways that nurture and care for others and the world (Elley-Brown and Pringle, 2019). It treats care as an organising principle.

Ethical childcare: care as an organising principle

What is ethical childcare? My proposed definition is that it is high-quality childcare which prioritises the needs of children above other factors, such as profit, the convenience of parents, practitioners or stakeholders, or compliance with government targets. It is also necessarily inclusive, which is a principle embedded in early years practice, but I extend this to mean that high-quality childcare and early years education should be affordable and accessible to all. Ethical childcare should also avoid exploiting practitioners, families, stakeholders and the natural world, by adopting ethical employment practices, ethical charging practices and environmentally sustainable working practices.

An ethic of care can help to define ethical childcare by recognising that ethical behaviour is rooted in a 'human affective response' (Noddings, 2013, p 3). An ethic of care encompasses all levels of influence within organisations, from political, economic and social forces down to the embodied nature of childcare practice. The recognition of ethical childcare can itself be a felt experience rather than a cognitive judgement, reflecting the affinity of care ethics in early years with a relational pedagogy of professional love (Page, 2018). The prevalent use of 'gut instinct' to judge a nursery, by both practitioners and parents, is echoed in the view of a high school teacher cited by Tronto (2010, p 159), who said that she could 'just tell' within ten minutes whether practitioners were caring. The link between care ethics, embodied care and tacit knowledge is something I explore in Chapter 7, leading to my model of ethical sensemaking.

The Care Collective's *Care Manifesto* called for care to be an organising principle 'on each and every scale of life' and for care and care practices to be understood as broadly as possible (Chatzidakis et al, 2020, p 20). I hope to contribute to that understanding in terms of care within early years care and education by applying an ethics of care perspective to childcare at all levels of influence, from the individual practice of practitioners to organisational policies and practice to government policies and societal influences. The *Care Manifesto*'s subtitle – *The Politics of Interdependence* – is also relevant to the ethics of care and childcare practice and to the process of schoolification. At the heart of an ethics of care is the recognition of a care need and the rejection of the idea that children and adults should strive to be independent, and this goes to the heart of respectful, caring childcare. Thankfully, the 'old-school' attitude in some nurseries of not picking up children who are struggling to settle 'because they have to get used to it' has now been widely recognised as both cruel and ineffective, but it stemmed from a belief that children needed to become emotionally as well as physically independent. The belief of a small segment of society that young children benefit from being sent to boarding schools is the extreme implementation of that misconception. A feminist ethic of care views individuals as relational and interdependent, rather than independent and self-sufficient (Held, 2006).

Tronto's four phases of care (set out first in Tronto, 1993) provide an illustration of how the issue of independence relates to an ethics of care, and why this should be a political as well as a personal concern. The first phase, 'caring about', involves the recognition of the need for care, which requires attentiveness, itself a moral concept, in not allowing suffering to be ignored. Seeing a child's distress or discomfort is an obvious trigger for practitioners to act, but recognising the need for families to be able to access affordable, high-quality childcare is a political issue. Recognising the need for caring employment practices and the need to empathise with families who might be struggling with balancing parenthood and work are organisational issues. Environmental policies arise when there is a recognition of the need for more care to be taken of the natural world, by governments, organisations and individuals.

The second phase, 'taking care of', describes the act of taking on responsibility for meeting the identified care need. When a child's key person in a nursery is absent, another practitioner needs to take on that responsibility, and if a parent leaves a child in a distressed state, it is often not only the child that will need comforting. A caring practitioner will also take responsibility for sending a reassuring message (ideally with a photo) to show the parent that their child has recovered quickly and is now enjoying their day at nursery. Nursery managers need to act when they observe practitioners struggling with a particularly challenging situation, those in positions of power need to ensure that employees are cared for, and politicians need to take responsibility for addressing the crisis of availability and affordability of high-quality childcare.

Tronto observed that the first two phases of care are the duties of the powerful, while the third and fourth are left to the less powerful. 'Caregiving', the third phase, is often deemed by society to be a private matter, but it also describes the work of childcare. The ethical aspect of caregiving draws attention to the importance of competence in caregiving. It is not sufficient to change babies' nappies efficiently and to keep children warm and safe. Highly competent caregivers recognise the need for emotional warmth and the provision of an environment that encourages babies' and young children's cognitive, social and physical development. Inadequate resources, understaffing and lack of training, for example, can result in caregiving not fully meeting the needs of those being cared for.

The fourth phase identified by Tronto is 'care-receiving'. This requires responsiveness by the carer, and this goes to the heart of the issue of interdependence. It is the feedback loop from a child's smiles and laughter that allows practitioners to recognise their success in comforting a distressed child, but it is also the feedback from parents about their child's development at home – for instance, when parents report that their child sings songs they've learned at nursery or tells them that paper should be recycled, not binned! It is, however, sometimes easy to assume that care is sufficient if no negative feedback is received, when skilled practitioners in fact need to learn to read body language and to ask verbal children for their feedback about help or care that is given to them. Employers, politicians and organisation leaders also need to proactively seek feedback on policies or actions that are intended to be caring in nature but which may be misguided. Tronto insisted that care-receiving is an important phase because it is the only way to know if caring needs have been met.

Twenty years after Tronto first set out these four phases of care, she proposed a fifth phase to embrace a democratic ideal of caring – that of 'caring with' (Tronto, 2013). This, she suggested, would help to create caring democracies that would allocate caring responsibilities, recognising that everyone is part of an ongoing system in which we may move between either end of the giving–receiving scale throughout our lives. The macro-level debate about how best to create caring democracies extends beyond the remit of this book, but an ethic of care can be applied in almost any situation, from policy to practice.

Practice theory can support this implementation by providing greater insight into the actions and behaviours that are involved in putting ethical theory into care practices. Tronto argued that there is 'a great danger in thinking of care as a commodity, as purchased services, rather than as a process' (2010, p 164), and Noddings (2002) developed a phenomenology of care, although she described it as a description of caring encounters rather than a Husserlian phenomenological analysis. She identified receptive attention as an essential characteristic of a caring encounter and detailed the 'motivational displacement' that occurs when, for example, a practitioner responds to a child's demand for attention. The practitioner has to empathise with and understand the child's need at that moment in order to decide on an appropriate response. Effective scaffolding of a child's learning depends on a practitioner's understanding of a child's ability, as does a recognition of a child's zone of proximal development (Vygotsky, 1978).

The key person approach: relationality in pedagogy

I mentioned at the end of the previous chapter my belief that a relational pedagogy is a natural approach for early years settings wishing to embed an ethic of care. A key person approach is one aspect of that, but it is also an essential element of ethical childcare practice. The key person approach is a requirement in the Early Years Foundation Stage framework, which uses the terminology of 'must' for mandatory requirements and 'should' for advisory elements (Department for Education, 2025a, p 4). 'Each child must be assigned a key person. Their role is to help ensure that every child's care is tailored to meet their individual needs, to help the child become familiar with the setting, offer a settled relationship for the child and build a relationship with their parents and/or carers' (Department for Education, 2025a, p 30). The key person approach has been recognised as an important feature of high-quality early years practice and it has its origins in attachment theory.

Attachment theory originated with Bowlby (1969), a psychoanalyst and psychiatrist, who recognised the importance of secure attachment for an infant's emotional well-being. A great deal of research has developed and amended Bowlby's original findings, including acknowledging their potentially Eurocentric bias and noting that attachment is not limited simply to a one-to-one infant–mother relationship, but that other attachment figures within the family and childcare settings are also important. Neurobiological research has shown that children who have secure attachment have higher levels of brain activity in areas crucial to empathy (Music, 2017), and secure attachment relationships are often formed in nurseries where emotional understanding is central to the philosophy and practices. In other nurseries, however, there is insufficient understanding of the benefits of developing attachment bonds in buffering anxiety levels of young children (Bowlby, 2007).

Caregiving has been described as an underdeveloped concept within attachment theory (Bell and Richard, 2000), partly ascribed to a lack of attention to motivation and emotion. Noddings' (1984) notion of ethical, rather than natural, care is helpful in understanding the motivation of early years professionals, and I discuss emotions in the next chapter, but Bell and Richard (2000) also described the way in which caring can be an enduring emotion that affects both parties and which can serve as an autonomous motivation. The joy expressed by a child on seeing their favourite adult within a nursery (who may not be their key person, but often is) is clearly going to elicit a positive emotion in the recipient of that joyful expression. The connection between the adult and child is thereby strengthened, and the adult's ethical motivation to care is rewarded. Caring for children will in itself generate affection and attachment. As Alison Gopnik summed up, '[w]e don't care for children because we love them; we love them because we care for them' – and even more succinctly, '"attachment" is the psychologist's name for "love"' (2016, pp 87, 117).

Attentive responses to the needs of children are facilitated by high staff–child ratios, low staff turnover and effective training of early years professionals, but that also means that the opposite has a negative impact. Contrary to Bowlby's studies, more recent research into the impact of cortisol suggests that 'affectionate, trusting relationships with a small group of adults who reliably care for them in a calm, attentive, affectionate fashion' is preferable to home environments that are impacted by unmanageable stress levels, often due to poverty (Jarvis, 2020, p 9). Attachment theory is an integral part of embedding an ethic of care through a key person approach, but it is important to recognise that it has a broader application than the original mother–child dyad, or 'limpet theory' as it has been called (Penn, 2019, p 44). The concept of professional love (Page, 2018) and a recognition that children can form relationships with several adults, as well as other children, is helpful for embedding an ethic of care that helps to develop children's emotional well-being, but an established and carefully nurtured key person approach, which recognises the need for secure attachments within an early years setting, is a critical foundation for caring, relational pedagogy.

Relational pedagogy describes the practices that encourage practitioners to engage in responsive, affectionate interactions with children (Howard et al, 2018) and to use their knowledge and understanding of a child's interests and level of development to ensure a curriculum that is child-centred and developmentally appropriate. Practitioners support children's curiosity and questioning, risk-taking and autonomy, and are able to tailor their support to individual children's needs. It underpins sustained shared thinking as well as emotional well-being, and perhaps most critically, it focuses on the process of learning, not outcomes (Papatheodorou, 2009), providing a more dynamic and reflective approach to learning that is more suitable to the fast-changing world we live in than any preconceived and static focus on 'school-readiness'.

'Not like a conveyor belt': care routines

Care routines include how children's self-care skills are supported, but also, I suggest, how the environment is cared for. A Danish example may provide a helpful comparison here. Jytte Juul Jensen (2011) described filmed examples, where the practice in an English childhood centre was seen as focusing on adult-directed learning, with mealtimes, sleep-times and toileting portrayed as interruptions to educational activities and, therefore, to be carried out as efficiently as possible. In contrast, Danish pedagogues involved the children in the whole mealtime experience, setting and clearing the tables, wiping up spills and allowing plenty of time and space for 'everyday life'. Here, helping a child to blow their nose, for example, is considered an important aspect of a pedagogue's work and not to be delegated to assistants. Jensen also explained the Danish concept of *kropslighed*, which can be described as embodiment (or physicality, according to Google Translate), and the importance for Danish pedagogy of children being allowed to express themselves physically, which also relates to the much greater emphasis in Denmark on being outdoors. She contrasted the informal relations and relative freedom that are encouraged in Danish settings with a much more limited use of outdoor space in England.

I believe that the picture painted by Jensen is now an outdated one that would only be true of some nurseries in England today. In most settings these days, practitioners are encouraged to sit with children at mealtimes, and children are involved in serving their own meals and to clear away afterwards. An examination of the routinisation of care practices in early years settings is helpful in understanding the impact of those routines on both children and practitioners. A new practitioner at one of the Acorn nurseries told me how her previous nursery had a timetable for nappy changing, with each practitioner taking it in turns to do whole groups of children in succession. I describe the implications of this, and how much it contrasts with an ideal nappy change, in the next chapter, but one of the effects of this 'conveyor belt' approach, in the words of some interviewees, is to mechanise, almost dehumanise, the care routine, in contrast to giving the responsibility and autonomy to practitioners to decide when their key children need their nappies changing.

Conversely, it does make sense to have a set time for children to have a sleep at nursery. This involves creating a period of calm relaxation for a whole group of children, usually after lunch, when they will be likely to be naturally sleepy after having eaten. How each child goes to sleep, and how long they need to sleep for, however, will vary according to the individual, so the sleep routine also needs effective communication between team members to share the key person's knowledge of a child's sleep preferences, recognising that lunch breaks may also mean that a child's key person is unlikely to be present for both the going-to-sleep routine and a child's waking up. Having an embedded ethic of care within a nursery would ensure that the needs of each child are prioritised, and this may also require skilful negotiation and liaison with families, whose preference for a child's sleep duration may pose a dilemma for practitioners if their perception of the child's needs is different – a situation I describe in Chapter 7 as an example of ethical sensemaking.

Early years theorists and their ideas

Table 4.2 presents key theorists in the early years field who have influenced the development of thought around education and care – particularly the kind of outdoor and relational pedagogy that characterised many of the settings included in my research that embraced an ethical, respectful ethic of care (though it was not necessarily named as such). Three of the eight were psychologists, reflecting the early interest in child development from a cognitive perspective. Of the educators, only the two women in the list were specifically interested in the early years age range, and both based their work on their own hands-on experience. Theorists focusing specifically on early years care and education came later, but the training and development of early years practitioners usually covers the work of the theorists in this list. Some ideas, like Piaget's stages of development, are now considered to be problematic in that they do not reflect more recent neuroscientific discoveries, but others, such as Froebel's and Montessori's ideas, have seen a renewal of interest in recent years, with their pedagogies widely adopted within the early years sector.

The thorny issue of quality in early years provision has been extensively explored, with two influential studies being the Effective Provision of Pre-School Education Project (Sylva et al, 2004) and the Study of Early Education and Development (Melhuish and Gardiner, 2018, updated 2021). All early years settings must comply with the standards set out in the Early Years Foundation Stage framework (Department for Education, 2025a); the curriculum and pedagogy followed by individual settings is not prescribed, although aspects such as sustained shared thinking (Siraj-Blatchford, 2009; Howard et al, 2018) are widely recognised as important features of high-quality provision. The autonomy of settings and early years professionals to devise their own curriculum is important. While I am reluctant to align good childcare with a specific pedagogy, my research interviews consistently illustrated the effectiveness of relational pedagogies when embedding an ethos of respectful care. Other approaches that appeared to facilitate an ethic of care were nature pedagogies, slow pedagogy and, to a certain extent, Reggio Emilia-influenced and Montessori nurseries, although the latter varied markedly, showing very different interpretations of a Montessori approach.

One consistent element of the early years theorists that resonates with an ethical approach is the recognition of the importance of play. Dewey (2020 [1922], p 80) described the 'immense moral importance of play'. Table 4.2 demonstrates the international range of the theorists' ideas and where they fit into the timescale of developing thought.

Table 4.2: Early years theorists

Name and dates	Nationality and profession	Main ideas
Friedrich Froebel (1782–1852)	German educator	Took a maternalist approach to childcare; invented the kindergarten and is purported to have said that 'play is the highest expression of human development in childhood'
John Dewey (1859–1952)	American philosopher, social psychologist, pragmatist and educational reformer	Saw education as a process of living and schools as social institutions; argued for progressive, experiential learning and the moral importance of play; explored the concept of habit; influenced sensemaking
Margaret McMillan (1860–1931)	Scottish nursery school pioneer and activist	Campaigned to improve children's health and education, including through provision of meals; early proponent of outdoor pedagogy
Rudolf Steiner (1861–1925)	Austrian social reformer and philosopher; founder of Waldorf schools	Founded spiritual-scientific 'anthroposophy', which focuses on freedom, imagination and creativity; influenced McMillan and the proponents of slow pedagogy
Maria Montessori (1870–1952)	Italian doctor and educator; founder of Montessori education	Part of the kindergarten movement; encouraged children to work and learn independently using specific didactic materials
Lev Vygotsky (1896–1934)	Russian psychologist	Put forward the sociocultural theory of development as socially mediated; developed the concept of the zone of proximal development
Jean Piaget (1896–1980)	Swiss psychologist	Put forward that children have four stages of cognitive development, in a fixed order
Loris Malaguzzi (1920–94)	Italian educational philosopher	Founded Reggio Emilia, a child-centred approach

5

Caring as an embodied practice in early years provision

The importance of touch

'In early childhood, the sensations of the body are the pathways to the child's thoughts, emotions, and attitudes' (Murray, 2021, p 66). There is increasing recognition of the importance of tactile experience for very young infants (Montagu, 1986), with the way we touch children having been described as 'our first and foundational language' (Murray, 2021, p 71). Babies and children in early years settings spend a lot of time in close physical contact during care practices, and they

> learn important ideas about self, others and relationships, according to the way educators physically handle, hold and touch them ... the adult's non-verbal communications of touch, eye contact and gesture, tell young children what the adult thinks and feels about them. They absorb the adult's feelings and attitudes into their bodies ... and internalise these messages into their developing sense of self. (Manning-Morton, 2024, p 109)

The importance of cuddling and stroking for children's socioemotional and physical well-being extends beyond infancy (Field, 2010), as touch is a basic behavioural need. When a child's need for affectionate touching is not met at home, it is even more critical that early years practitioners are able to recognise and meet that need. Touch is an important aspect of ethical childcare practices, as is the need for early years practitioners to be aware of how important it is for children to feel socioemotionally secure when at nursery and of the factors that might influence that.

The importance of touch for babies and toddlers cannot be overstated. The effects of tactile deprivation are well documented, not just from the poor monkeys in Harlow's experiments (Harlow et al, 1965), who preferred clinging to a cloth model of a mother than one made from wire, even when the wire mother was the one that provided milk, but as far back as the 13th century and the experiments of Frederick II, emperor of Germany, on babies. He forbade their foster mothers from engaging in any interaction with them, other than addressing their basic care needs, and the historian of the time noted that they all died 'for they could not live without the petting' (quoted in Montagu, 1986, p 102). Hundreds of years later, in 1928, advice to 'never hug and kiss them, never let them sit in your lap' came from a professor of psychology (quoted in Montagu, 1986, p 150) who adopted a behaviourist approach which is still alive today in the parenting advice of Tanya Byron, Gina Ford and Christopher Green, particularly around the idea that babies can be 'trained' to sleep in a separate bed. I'm not suggesting that the modern-day behaviourists are as uncaring as the notorious Truby King, whose rigid regimes caused immense distress for a whole generation of mothers and babies, as well as jeopardising any chance of successful breastfeeding, but they follow in that tradition.

In contrast, neurophysiologists today have proven the benefits of caring, tactile care, from the kangaroo care for premature babies to the recognition that the skin-to-skin sensory experience is important for a close relationship with an infant, ensuring they thrive (Norman, 2019). The growth in popularity of baby massage classes reflects the increased awareness of the role of touch in bonding, and there have been widespread reports of increased stress and depression caused by the enforced social distancing during the COVID-19 pandemic. The physical acts of childcare have tangible impacts on parents and carers, with hands-on fathers having lower levels of testosterone than fathers not involved in their child's day-to-day care. Perhaps the most dramatic impact, though, is on children's brain development and well-being. Touch is a 'primary predictor of children's sustained expression of positive emotions' (All-Party Parliamentary Group on a Fit and Healthy Childhood, 2020, p 25), and the research shows that therapeutic touch (C-tactile afferent, to use the clinical term) is particularly effective in contributing to the well-being of children who have experienced adversity.

So what does all this mean for the world of early years, and childcare practice in particular? Touch is one aspect of how care practices are embodied. Children are naturally tactile and enjoy cuddles from carers as well as family members. Early years practitioners are usually skilled at enabling children to have one-to-one physical reassurance in the course of a busy day and often wish for an extra pair of arms to be able to comfort more than one child at once. Sleep-time in nurseries is often facilitated by gentle stroking, and practitioners position themselves whenever they can at the child's level and within easy reach of children who may want to be reassured by physical contact. But there are different kinds of touch. There's a tangible difference between functional touch and the kind of pleasant touch that releases oxytocin, and the significance of touch in early years practice can be seen in the myriad ways in which touch forms part of an everyday care routine, which are too often carried out on autopilot and, I believe, can be missed opportunities to transmit warmth and love to receptive infants.

The care routines I mean include nose-wiping, nappy changing and cleaning children after meals and messy activities. In Chapter 2, I recounted the example of the training session run by Cara, a nursery manager, with her team, using wet flannels to illustrate the difference in cleansing with a caring touch and cold, efficient cleansing without a caring touch. The participants described their hands feeling different as a result of two contrasting experiences, and hopefully they took that new sensory awareness into their next care routine. Another example arose in one of the Acorn nurseries when a new team member put on vinyl gloves before putting suncream on the children's faces and arms. Her colleagues expressed dismay, and she explained that in her previous setting, a school nursery, that was the required protocol. The discussion that ensued among the team focused on how it would feel to have cream applied with plastic-gloved hands and the medicalising impression that gave.

Similarly, nappy changing times are unlikely to be a highlight of any early years practitioner's day, but they are one of the few guaranteed one-to-one moments between a child and their key person and involve intimate care. Safeguarding begins on the changing mat. Toddlers learn that only trusted adults should be allowed to remove their clothes and touch their intimate areas. This is why it's important that key persons or their buddies should be the ones doing the nappy changing, rather than there being a 'conveyor belt' approach with staff taking it in turns to do several nappies at set times. Apart from anything else, a key person gets to know a child's toileting habits (what is 'normal' for one child might be considered a loose nappy for another) and their preferences – favourite songs or rhymes, or a toy to hold to discourage a 'helping hand' reaching down. Caring practitioners will also do their best to make sure their hands aren't cold.

Feeding is probably one of the most critical care routines needing a caring touch. Babies who are being bottle-fed need a nurturing cuddle and eye contact just as much as the nutritional value of the milk. Practitioners are spared the distraction of smartphones while feeding, but they also need to be able to focus on their task without being distracted by their colleagues and other children – it's a precious one-to-one time that often precedes sleep-time for the infant. I was very impressed by an account from Amy, who had the confidence to challenge an Ofsted inspector who tried to engage her in a conversation while she was feeding a baby: 'I said, "I'm just gonna stop you there." I had to explain to her. I said: "I'm going to give him a bottle, then I'm gonna put him to bed, and then I'll be with you." She went "Oh all right, yes, yes."' Amy's approach of prioritising the needs of her charge over the demands of an Ofsted inspector demonstrated her professional autonomy and agency as well as being an example of her awareness of the importance of attentive care.

Such attentiveness is a key aspect of an ethic of care, and one that is endangered by the ubiquity of smartphones and other media, and while nurseries sometimes struggle to provide the individual attention that babies and toddlers thrive on, they are also in the privileged position of being freed from the competing domestic and work demands that many parents at home are faced with. The widely replicated 'still face' experiment, introduced by Edward Tronick in 1975, provides a dramatic demonstration of the importance of warm communication between carer and infant. It shows the reaction of an infant whose mother initially interacts with her child but then becomes expressionless and non-responsive. The child becomes confused, attempts to connect with her mother and then becomes distressed and finally gives up trying to re-engage. The impact was the same when the experiment was conducted with fathers and would probably also apply within childcare settings.

Finally, touch in early years practice illustrates the ways in which care is embodied. Most parents feel nervous and awkward handling their first newborn, but soon learn the most comfortable and comforting way to hold and soothe their baby. Early years practitioners, too, soon learn the importance of body language, facial expressions, gestures, tone of voice and body positioning for generating a rapport with children. There is a set of skills in childcare that cannot be articulated, as well as tacit knowledge that is embodied and learned through practical experience. It's a profession in which it is absolutely an advantage to have had parenting experience. That's not to say that training and qualifications aren't important. For example, professional discourse about Leuven's 'levels of involvement' (Laevers, 1994) when observing children can identify situations where more can be done to nurture and develop children's social and emotional development and spot potential areas for concern. Children can be very good at demanding attention, but practitioners have to be equally skilled at noticing those in need of attention but not demonstrating that need verbally or physically.

A child needs to know that someone in their environment is there for them and that their physical need for touch and reassurance will never be rejected. Nursery manager Helen had several children with chaotic home environments, and she described her pride in how her team had supported children who had witnessed distressing violence at home, commenting that 'they might not be writing, but they're not panicking every time someone makes a loud noise. They can go to an adult and have a hug and be okay ... we get there in the end.' Early years settings can't solve wider social problems, but they can offer a caring, nurturing environment that enables children to feel safe and loved, and an awareness of the importance of touch is an essential ingredient in this. The way in which the word 'touch' is used in other contexts, such as being 'touched' emotionally or being 'in touch', emphasises the communicative aspect of touch, both literally and metaphorically. The philosopher Diderot asserted that of all the senses, touch is 'the most profound and philosophical' (quoted in Paterson, 2007, p 1).

Tacit knowledge and embodied care

Early years practitioners are not always able to articulate the knowledge and skills that inform their practice, as they rely on expertise that has become intuitive and normative. This kind of sensory awareness is something that can be explored through the concept of tacit knowledge. Froebel's ideal teacher in the form of a 'mother made conscious' (Steedman, 1985) links the idea of tacit knowledge back to the maternalism described in the previous chapter. Benjamin Spock, the well-known American paediatrician, challenged the rigid scheduling of the behaviourist school of Truby King and others, and the opening lines of his influential *Common Sense Book of Baby and Child Care* encourage parents to rely on their own instinctive, tacit knowledge: 'Trust yourself. You know more than you think you do' (Spock and Parker, 1998, p 1). Tacit knowledge was first developed as a concept by Polanyi, who called 'the area where the tacit predominates to the extent that articulation is virtually impossible … the *ineffable domain*' (1958, p 87, emphasis in original).

The idea was further developed and challenged by management theorists Nonaka and Takeuchi (1995), who put forward a model for converting tacit knowledge into explicit knowledge to facilitate its communication for others to learn. Treating tacit and explicit knowledge as two distinct types of knowledge in this way has been described as a conversion perspective (Hadjimichael and Tsoukas, 2019), but this knowledge creation model has been criticised for trying to operationalise and articulate something that is 'essentially inarticulable' (Polanyi, 1958, p 60), and as Tsoukas suggests instead: 'New knowledge comes about not when the tacit becomes explicit, but when our skilled performance – our praxis – is punctuated in new ways by social interaction' (2002, p 426). This approach sees a practice perspective as having three distinguishing features: the mutually constituted nature of tacit and explicit knowledge, the inseparability of tacit knowledge and sociomateriality and the importance of embodiment. These features resonate with the world of early years and can easily be applied to childcare practices.

First, the inseparability of tacit and explicit knowledge can be seen in the experience of many nursery managers and mentors who find that instruction and role-modelling are often insufficient to influence the practice of others and that ongoing professional reflection and discussion is needed alongside role-modelling to improve awareness of the often-unconscious details of childcare practices. Peer observations that are accompanied by video recordings can lead to moments of revelation when practitioners see for themselves their body positioning, movements and tone of voice. Tacit knowledge within early years practice includes how best to comfort children in distress and how to build rapport and gain cooperation when needed, illustrating the relational nature of some tacit knowledge. In the following, Paula, a mature nursery assistant, reflected on what she had learned from caring for her own children in terms which resonate for many early years practitioners, although it is now recognised that being 'tuned in' to a child's needs is the result of spending time caring for children, rather than the result of becoming a parent:

> I think when you've been a mum, you know when they're not right, and you have that instinct. I think when you become a mum, you then change and see things differently … it's like you're more tuned in to the children. So you look out for when they're hungry, they're thirsty, like, they need that little bit of extra attention. And, yeah, your senses become more heightened, I think.

All children are unique – it is never one size fits all. And tacit knowledge can include how to 'read' a child's needs, particularly at the preverbal stage.

The embodied nature of tacit knowledge is particularly relevant for early years practitioners, and Hamington's concept of embodied care is helpful in examining this more closely. Hamington (2004) describes embodied care as consisting of three interrelated aspects (see Figure 5.1). The first of these, 'caring knowledge', recognises knowledge as being 'sensible' (see Gherardi, 2012) as well as collective, situated and socially constructed. Hamington calls on the phenomenological argument of Merleau-Ponty, which holds that the body plays a part in both acquiring knowledge and creating meaning. An early years practitioner learns how to handle babies and toddlers by gaining experience and by learning the differences between individuals. One baby may be passive and compliant and another a bundle of raw energy, wriggling incessantly. Only by getting to know the infant can a practitioner learn to identify whether the wriggling is down to joyful exuberance or frustration. One toddler may express their discomfort at loud noises in the room by clinging to a practitioner for physical reassurance, while another may withdraw into a quiet corner.

'Caring imagination' is the second of Hamington's three aspects of embodied care, and he links this to empathy, which he traces back to Adam Smith's and David Hume's sympathetic approach to moral imagination – though the term 'empathy' was not used until the 20th century (Slote, 2007). Hamington's perspective on empathy is that it is crucial in extending the boundary of care beyond those with whom we are familiar, and he notes the similarity with Noddings' distinction between natural and ethical caring: 'for Noddings, ethical caring involves reflection and decision' (Hamington, 2004, p 68). He discusses critical reflection as a further aspect of caring imagination, using the example of a parent balancing potentially conflicting demands for a child's protection and autonomy, which is a dilemma familiar to early years practitioners, particularly with the increased awareness of the importance of 'risky play' (Gill, 2007; Sandseter, 2009; Kingston-Hughes, 2022).

Figure 5.1: Hamington's aspects of embodied care

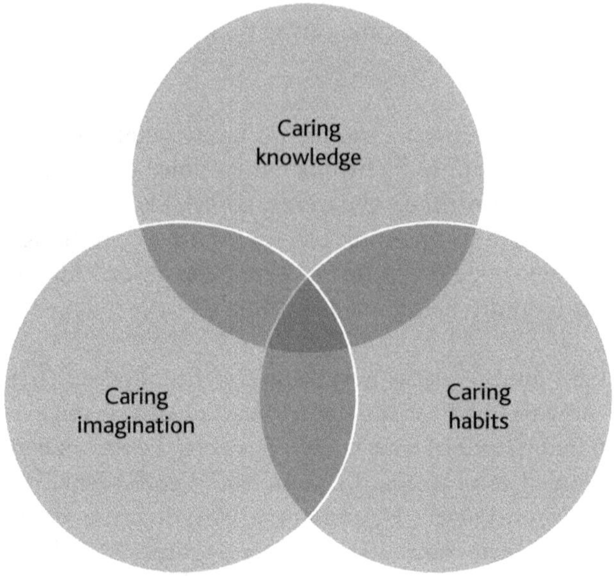

[Venn diagram with three overlapping circles labelled "Caring knowledge", "Caring imagination", and "Caring habits"]

Source: Based on Hamington (2004)

The third aspect of embodied care discussed by Hamington, 'caring habits', is, I feel, the area which has the strongest argument for care being embodied. Hamington argues that 'attending to and reinforcing the habits of care can inculcate a caring disposition' and that 'habit is a type of embodied knowledge' (2004, pp 85, 56). This brings us back to the concept of tacit knowledge and the bodily habits and skills of soothing distressed children through the deft but gentle physical care routines of changing nappies, dressing and helping to wipe noses or clean hands and faces. New parents consciously learn care techniques, and the methods used become habitual over a period of time; the same applies to new early years practitioners, whose care practice habits are learned in their first few years of experience. Hamington (2004, p 58) also highlights the 'intertwining of embodied and cognitive knowledge' in situations where children may exhibit distress for trivial reasons (not being allowed to help themselves to sweets in a supermarket, for example).

Dealing with distressed children when the distress is perceived to be unreasonable is where childcare practice enters the field of moral dilemmas. It is also an area where poor caring habits come to light – whether a child's distress is acknowledged or dismissed and whether sufficient allowance is made for a young child's inability to self-regulate their emotions. Active listening, a social habit of care that Hamington ascribes to the work of Jane Addams in particular, is a key feature of ethical early years practice. The importance of cuddles for children's levels of oxytocin is widely known by early years academics, and by many practitioners, and researchers have recognised the importance of 'how' rather than 'what' care is given (Langford and Richardson, 2020). As an example of a caring habit, Hamington provides an account of how he reacts if his daughter hurts herself and cries:

> I comfort her by hugging her body. This is not a habit in the sense of a repeated motion such as typing, but my body has captured the subtle movements necessary to communicate care. My arms do not squeeze her forcefully, as if I were holding a fifty-pound sack of potatoes ... My arms gently caress in a manner that reflect the concern and affection appropriate for the moment. I move into her personal space and apply just the right amount of pressure with my hands and arms to pull her close to my chest. The hug may last only seconds, and few words may pass between us, but important knowledge is transferred. My daughter and I will not consciously attend to all the subtleties of the physical movement. These movements are not overdetermined. My habits of care take on a certain disposition and tone ... My tone of voice will reflect my concern. In addition, I not only communicate care but also model a habit that her body catches. (Hamington, 2004, p 57)

Hamington then asserts the longer-term impact of this caring habit:

> If she is exposed to this model of caring repeatedly, she will likely employ this habit when confronted with a similar circumstance. In this manner habits of care pass embodied knowledge from parent to child. (Hamington, 2004, p 57)

Such a transfer of caring habits takes place in nurseries too, and an awareness of these positive caring habits highlights the potential impact of their absence. In some cases, when the lack of responsiveness is continual, and associated with other types of neglect, it may be characterised as adverse childhood experiences, which can have a severely detrimental impact on a child's well-being. A poignant example described by Music (2017) shows the different reactions of securely attached children and children who had not experienced attuned parenting when shown two different scenarios. In the first, a mother and baby climbed up some steps and when the baby couldn't keep up and began crying, the mother returned, but in the second, the baby was just left. The securely attached children showed evident surprise in the second case, whereas the insecure children had the opposite response, being more surprised when the mother returned in response to the baby's cry. Expectations of caring reactions clearly depend on experience.

Another feature of high-quality childcare practice that relies on tacit knowledge and caring habits is one which Hamington traces back to

Merleau-Ponty's phenomenology of the body – in particular, his emphasis on perception. As Hamington argues, embodied perception can help to create unconscious caring habits. Being able to perceive subtle changes in children's behaviour or emotional state can be a key aspect of responsiveness, which can help to develop a sense of others' needs – particularly helpful when working with children who may not be able to articulate their emotional or physical feelings. It enables complexity and subtlety in caring responses and can be a mixture of articulated knowledge as well as tacit corporeal understanding. This embodied knowledge is evident in caring interactions and can easily be seen in the way skilful practitioners position themselves in relation to the children in their care in ways which allow tactile as well as vocal reassurance and responsiveness for unsettled or distressed children. The extent to which caring habits are conscious or tacit will probably vary between practitioners and is likely to be more evident in situations where there are barriers to effective caring. Sociopolitical factors and structural factors, such as staffing levels, have been observed to hinder the implementation of care ethics in early years settings (Langford and Richardson, 2020). There is also a potential artistry to consider; caregivers have been described as 'artists in terms of being aesthetically attuned to the bodies, actions, and relations of themselves and others' (Hamington, 2015, p 279), with a performative aspect that helpfully emphasises the embodied nature of care.

The embodied and sociomaterial nature of tacit knowledge has been described as 'indwelling' (Hadjimichael and Tsoukas, 2019; Hadjimichael et al, 2023), and this concept is particularly helpful for understanding the ways in which skilled and experienced practitioners develop a deftness in care practices which becomes unconscious competence, allowing their attention to focus on a child's body language and emotions, not just on their physical needs. Regular car drivers reach a level of expertise that means they no longer have to apply the same conscious attention to change gear, regulate speed, check mirrors and indicate that they did when learning to drive. In the same way, an experienced early years practitioner will know how best to handle a wriggling child who needs their wet clothing changed and how to use a range of verbal modulations and facial expressions to capture the interest of children when reading them a story. It also means that the acquisition of caring habits is a critical factor in determining whether being on autopilot results in caring or uncaring care practices.

Fortunately, working in early years settings is rarely mundane in the implementation of regular activities, as children are all different and are likely to react differently to every activity. Familiarity with a story, and knowledge of the children's level of interest and familiarity with it, can be used to inform the pace of storytelling and to gauge the amount of dialogic interaction that will extend the children's vocabulary, understanding and other pre-reading skills without spoiling the enjoyment of the narrative.

When the storytelling is 'second nature' and the practitioner is 'indwelling' with the use of the book and their own body as props, he or she is able to monitor the children's attentiveness and adjust pace and narrative accordingly.

Storytelling also provides an example of the social roots of tacit knowledge, or what Polanyi (1958) calls 'conviviality'. The narrative structure of songs and rhymes offers early opportunities for babies and toddlers to participate in the experience. My grandson was less than a year old when he began to scream excitedly in anticipation every time anyone began singing 'row, row, row your boat', as the version he was familiar with ended with 'don't forget to scream'. As children become more familiar with favourite stories, they eagerly anticipate favourite passages or endings. When I read my two-year-old granddaughter her favourite book (*Goldilocks and the Three Crocodiles* by Michael Rosen), she anticipated the page where the crocodiles first appeared by turning her head away for a few seconds, every time, as if they were too scary to contemplate. Such reactions can be contagious in a group situation, often adding to the enjoyment and drama of a story. Early years settings have a wealth of traditions and communication practices that often become part of a daily routine for both practitioners and children. Songs and rhymes with actions offer early participative experiences for children, and regularly used phrases are soon mimicked by children as they develop their language skills, highlighting the importance of professionalism and a warm emotional environment within settings.

The politics of breastfeeding: the ultimate in embodied care

What does breastfeeding have to do with care ethics? More, perhaps, than you might imagine. Breastfeeding is widely acknowledged as providing the best nutritional start for babies, lowering the risk of many long-term health issues and providing increased immunity to viruses and infections. It also has physiological and emotional benefits for those mothers who succeed at a practice which can be as challenging as it is 'natural'. When maternity leave is shortened for economic reasons, or because no paid leave is available, as is the case for 81 per cent of American parents (Wuori, 2024), it is even more difficult to establish breastfeeding. Extending paid maternity leave has been shown to have a direct impact on whether mothers decide to try breastfeeding, on whether they breastfeed exclusively and on the duration of breastfeeding (Chai et al, 2018). The World Health Organization (2023) recommends exclusive breastfeeding, on demand, for the first six months of life and, ideally, breastfeeding continuing over the first two years. But although breastfeeding rates in England have increased in recent years, only 53 per cent of infants are still breastfed at six to eight weeks, according to the Nuffield Trust (2024, as of 2023–24, based on the QualityWatch indicator).

Most nurseries in the UK are happy to accept and feed babies with expressed breast milk, but the additional effort for working mothers of expressing milk is daunting and to some extent negates one of the joys of breastfeeding, which is that, for a while at least, there is no need to bother with the complicated and expensive business of bottle-feeding. Breastfeeding within nurseries is usually confined to practitioners with their own babies or mothers who visit their babies during their lunch hour or at pick-up time. Early years professionals certainly become adept at bottle-feeding, and, sadly, I've heard a few comments over the years along the lines of 'I probably won't bother with breastfeeding, as I'd rather stick to what I know.' Breastfeeding as a practice, however, is the model for infant feeding that practitioners emulate in the practice of bottle-feeding. The cuddling in the body positioning, the eye contact and the opportunity for quiet soothing words characterise an optimally nurturing practice. Conversely, babies being fed propped up or holding their own bottle, or being fed while the practitioner's attention is elsewhere, represent a lack of caring attentiveness and miss a precious opportunity for a bonding moment.

But why is this 'politics'? The answer is that the practice of breastfeeding has been subject to interference by commercial interests and by a (usually male) misguided focus on quantity and routinisation, which results in a loss of confidence in the mother attempting to breastfeed. There are many reasons why so many women struggle to breastfeed or decide not to try, not all of which relate to the prospect of returning to work, although an early return to work, as a result of economic pressures, is certainly one of the barriers. In addition, there are often physical difficulties for new mothers, particularly first-time mothers, who may have received only limited information about what to expect, how to master the latching on and positioning, and how to have confidence that a baby is receiving enough milk. In other times and cultures, breastfeeding may have been more visible and familiar, but for many first-time mothers now, the first time they see it taking place is their own first attempt to latch their baby on.

The inevitable marketing of bottles and sterilisers may also unwittingly undermine confidence in a mother's ability to breastfeed, and although shared parenting is absolutely the optimum situation, and to be encouraged, it can influence parents to introduce bottle feeds very early on in order to give other parents and carers the opportunity to be involved in a baby's feeding. In a world where data gathering is an increasingly normalised part of day-to-day life, with smartphones and watches counting steps and various other actions, there is inevitably an appeal for anxious parents in the easily measured quantities of milk when bottle-feeding, in contrast to the embodied experience of breastfeeding, which relies more on attuning to a baby's body language and a mother's own perception of her milk supply.

The intense attachment that is often experienced between a breastfeeding mother and her baby can itself be a source of tension for new parents. Well-meaning family members and partners can easily undermine a mother's confidence in her ability to provide sufficient milk if the baby appears unsettled or is feeding frequently, particularly when compared to bottle-fed babies, who take longer to digest formula milk. Although most new mothers in the UK will take several months of maternity leave, many will also start to worry about how their baby will cope when they return to work, and introducing a bottle may be perceived as a sensible measure even though it may interfere with successful breastfeeding. On the mother's return to work, if the baby is placed in a day nursery with a staff team of experienced bottle feeders, they may not know how to provide support for breastfeeding. Many parents choose a nursery that is convenient for both parents to share the dropping off and picking up, and with few nurseries situated within workplaces, most breastfeeding mothers are unlikely to be able to visit their child to breastfeed during work breaks, or they may not be encouraged to do so by their workplace or the nursery, even if it is logistically possible.

Breastfeeding is the quintessence of embodied care. Successful breastfeeding is dependent on a mother's hormones triggering the let-down reflex, and in her insightful memoir of motherhood, Anne Enright explains the unconscious and uncontrollable nature of this:

> The reflex is designed to work at the sight, sound, or thought of your baby – which is spooky enough – but the brain doesn't seem to know what a baby is, exactly, and so tries to make you feed anything helpless, or wonderful, or small. So I have let down milk for Russian submariners and German tourists dying on Concorde. Loneliness and technology get me every time, get my milk every time. Desire, also, stabs me not in the heart but on either side of the heart – but I had expected this. What I had not expected was that there should be some things that do not move me, that move my milk. Or that, sometimes, I only realise that I am moved when I feel the pain. I find myself lapsed into a memory I cannot catch, I find myself trying to figure out what it is in the room that is sad or lovely – was it that combination of words, or the look on his face? – what it is that has such a call on my unconscious attention, or my pituitary, or my alveolar cells. (2004, p 54)

'Unconscious attention' captures the nature of embodied care beautifully.

Breastfeeding, when it goes well, is of enormous psychological benefit to working mothers and their babies in the first two years, even when it has been reduced to night feeds or when a baby or toddler is unwell. There is no dispute about the enormous health benefits of breastfeeding, and in the context of a baby starting nursery, the additional immunity from breast milk is particularly invaluable. The unique bonding experience for breastfeeding mothers and their babies is also a more holistic benefit, providing a precious and restful time for mother and baby to reunite and be physically and emotionally close after a day at work and nursery. An ethic of care that focuses on the emotional, physical and psychological needs of the mother as well as the baby or toddler would certainly support and encourage breastfeeding whenever practical.

Ultimately, though, we also need to recognise the importance of the cultural context of breastfeeding. As Virginia Held observes:

> There is no more reason to think of human nursing as simply biological than it is to think this way of, say, a businessman's lunch. Eating is a biological process, but what and how and with whom we eat are thoroughly cultural. Whether and how long and with whom a woman nurses an infant are also human, cultural matters. If men transcend the natural by conquering new territory and trading with their neighbours and making deals over lunch to do so, women can transcend the natural by choosing not to nurse their children when they could, or choosing to nurse them when their culture tells them not to, or singing songs to their infants as they nurse, or nursing in restaurants to overcome the prejudice against doing so, or thinking human thoughts as they do so, and so forth. Human culture surrounds and characterizes the activity of nursing as it does the activities of eating or governing or writing or thinking. (1993, p 54)

Emotions in childcare practice

One final aspect of embodiment in childcare practice is the way in which the tactile nature of the work can be seen as providing fulfilling emotional attachments for practitioners, which can then influence the quality of the emotional environment within the nursery (Boyer et al, 2013). Emotional attachments come with a health warning for practitioners, however. They may offer job fulfilment but also tie them into working arrangements that abuse their professionalism. Power relations are not unidirectional, and 'emotional stickiness' (Roberts-Holmes and Moss, 2021) also applies to parents, meaning parental choice as a policy is 'fundamentally flawed' (Gallagher, 2017) as the normal kind of consumer choice in a market transaction is thwarted by the emotional investment parents make in their child's childcare arrangements.

The concept of emotional labour refers to the commodification of emotions in customer-facing roles (Hochschild, 2012), and this resonates with the early years sector, as there is often a need for practitioners to appear calmer and happier than they may feel. The phenomenological experience of faking cheerfulness is not necessarily exploitative in the context of early years care and education, however, as practitioners can derive satisfaction by being a source of comfort for children, and the feeling of being needed, and of being effective in a caring role, can increase self-esteem (Isenbarger and Zembylas, 2006). The emotional demands on early years professionals are recognised as 'intense' in an All-Party Parliamentary Group report, which also highlights the dangers of inadequate support for practitioners, potentially resulting in them seeking to avoid children's demands, or becoming 'blind' to them (All-Party Parliamentary Group on a Fit and Healthy Childhood, 2020, p 32).

The ethical dimension of emotional labour in early years settings potentially arises in terms of the employer–employee relationship and in coping with infants and children in distress. Practitioners who see their vocation as a calling may suffer emotional distress in tolerating poor pay and conditions in order to continue supporting children and families who are dependent on them. This may have a negative impact on their own families, particularly when they are working long shifts to help maintain mandatory staffing ratios, and this raises the question of whether practitioners' families should be more visible stakeholders (Anastasiadis and Zeyen, 2022). 'Professional love' (Page, 2018) is a term that has been used to describe the ways in which practitioners employ emotions within their work with children. Whether this is seen as a kind of performative professionalism (Taggart, 2011) or a more fundamental requirement for early years practitioners to adopt, there is increasing neuroscientific evidence that infants and children have a fundamental need for carers who are attentive and that their emotional security depends more on the kind of care they receive in their early years than on any innate temperament.

A further problematic aspect of emotions in childcare practice is in the risk of emotions being perceived as unprofessional and, therefore, to be rejected, whereas I would argue that emotional warmth is a critical feature of attentive care and that a lack of emotion can lead to a lack of empathy and ethical slippage. Emotions carry risks, but there is a professionalism in managing emotions through self-regulation, which is a critical skill that can help early years professionals to also support children to develop their own self-regulation. Parents inevitably have an intense emotional involvement with their children, and this shouldn't be undermined. As Frank Furedi (2001) argues, parenting has been transformed from an intimate relationship involving emotion and warmth into a perception that technical skills are required and that parents may need to be educated about how best to bring up their children. Unfortunately, as he observes, 'projects that aim to transform incompetent adults into skilled parents have the unintended consequence of disempowering mothers and fathers and empowering the professionals' (2001, p 162). Parental instincts to pick up crying babies were demonised by behaviourists like Truby King, who advocated rigid routines, and even now there is still a multitude of so-called parenting experts whose advice is to ignore the distress of both parent and child in the efforts to 'train' babies to go to sleep on their own.

Supporting children to develop self-regulation is an immensely important aspect of early years practice, but many parents have similar struggles with their own emotional regulation. Several of my interviewees described challenging encounters with parents who struggled with self-regulation of emotions, often because they themselves had been in care or had experienced domestic abuse or other difficulties. Cara described a parent whose reaction to discovering that her child's key person was off sick was to create 'quite a hullabaloo for the child'. Cara followed up with a phone call to the parent 'and just said, you know, "How are you feeling?" and she said, "Oh, I'm so sorry, I'm so embarrassed."' Cara then commented: 'I think we've got to understand that parents, you know, sometimes parents haven't gone through this process themselves'; here, Cara demonstrated an understanding and an ethic of care, whereas others may have simply felt disgruntled and resentful about the parent's unreasonable reaction to the absence of her child's key person. Other interviewees observed that nursery practitioners are often seen as a 'safe middle ground' between friends, family and social services and that parents therefore often confide in them to an uncomfortable extent. Recognising and meeting the emotional needs of children and parents is one of the challenges of the role of an early years professional, but recognising the need to support colleagues with their emotions is equally important, as is seeing the positive value of emotional responses in developing genuinely caring responsiveness.

Care 'is a dimension of love', according to bel hooks, with the principles of a 'love ethic' comprising 'care, respect, knowledge, integrity, and the will to cooperate' (2001, p 100). All of these would just as easily comprise an ethic of care in early years practice, as well as Page's professional love. It has also been noted that 'caring in its purest form is not ordinary loving; it is doing spontaneously whatever the situation demands' (Dreyfus and Dreyfus, 1991, p 246). Geoff Taggart observes that the kind of professional love that infuses caring early years practice can be seen as 'expressions of innate *ethical nature as human beings*' (2019, p 98, emphasis in original).

The feel of time

Cara, a nursery manager with an avowed ethos of respectful care described her team's approach to care routines, detailing the way in which they are carried out:

> We put a lot of effort into our care routines and we prepare for them. We don't go and pick up a child from behind and they don't know

we're coming, going 'right we're changing your nappy' and walk off. We go to them, we go down to their level, we offer them, we ask them, we ask for permission to interact, to pick them up or whatever the interaction is we're going to do, and we listen, it's reciprocal. So lots of people ask children in care routines for their perspective, [but] they don't listen. In listening takes more time. You have to wait for a response from the person you're interacting with. So that is important.

'Listening takes more time' captures the need for a slower pace if children's needs are to be met effectively. Pace is a critical factor in nursery routines, and Cara's determination not to rush children was similarly applied to the post-lunch routine:

It's not rushed down from the table at lunch … it's in their time, it's unhurried, the member of staff gives themself 100 per cent to that child in that prime time. They're not going to be talking to other staff about, you know, where's the paper towels, or what time are you on your lunch break – it is devoting yourself 100 percent to be in that moment with that child. And so it maybe they've had a bottle together, they've sat together, they have some calm time together, and then they go towards the bed.

Pace is an ethical issue in day nursery routines, and although it depends on practitioners being sensitive to the negative impact on children of rushing care routines, it is also affected by organisational factors of staff shifts, staff ratios and session times. Staffing levels have a direct impact on pace. If, as in Cara's example, a practitioner is concerned with restocking paper towels, they have less time to focus on the children. There are mandatory minimum staff-to-child ratios, but if there are no ancillary roles, such as housekeepers, to undertake or help with the basic tasks of laundry, clearing up after children's meals or ongoing cleaning of toilet areas and replenishing hygiene supplies, the reality in many nurseries is that practitioners are expected to do these tasks alongside their care of the children. Being with small children for prolonged periods of time has been described as requiring 'working at different economies of scale and different spatio-temporal frameworks' (Baraister, 2009, p 129).

Childcare involves continually being alert to danger (a child choking at snack or mealtimes, climbing on furniture, injuring themselves or others, showing signs of serious illness) as well as balancing the needs of different children. It also entails undertaking the essential tasks involved in children's care and development, recording significant moments or times of sleep, nappy changes or details of food and drink, and noticing when a child is tired, thirsty or unhappy, particularly when they are too young to verbalise their needs. Assisting children to dress appropriately to go outside or to clean up after a toileting accident can take a frustrating amount of time when practitioners are pulled in different directions, so it can be counterintuitive to hold back from doing the task for them. Allowing time for children to learn the skills of putting arms in sleeves and doing up zips is a nurturing, caring act when it is done with verbal encouragement and patience, but it does take time, which can be a scarce resource if nurseries are short-staffed.

When a child joins a nursery, there is usually a settling-in process which is, ideally, adapted to the needs of the child and the family. The purpose of settling-in visits is to familiarise a child with the practitioners and the nursery environment before being left for the first time, which would usually not be for a full session, but would be increased gradually in line with the child's growing ease at being there. Occasionally, nurseries adopt a more rigid approach; one nursery website stipulates that their two-hour settling in sessions, during which the parents must stay with the child, 'are held up to twice a week, they are provided free of charge over a one- or two-week period'. The implication of this timescale is that after this maximum of four visits with a parent, full fees are paid for each session a child attends, so there is no offer to leave a child for an hour or two initially, to allow them to settle in more gradually – if a parent is having to pay for a full session, that can act as an incentive for them to use the whole session, whether or not their child would benefit from shorter sessions initially. An ethical approach, I suggest, would place a child's needs above the drive to begin charging full fees as quickly as possible. It is, of course, a balancing act for a nursery that may be struggling to maintain financial viability, but rushing the settling-in process can backfire and delay the development of a child's emotional security.

Time has been described as a precondition for ethical care (Fisher and Tronto, 1990), recognising that skills and knowledge are insufficient if caregivers do not have sufficient time to apply them. Alison Clark (2023) argues the benefits of slow pedagogies but also expresses the view that the problems that arise from 'accelerated childhood' are more fundamental than simply the need to take time to care for children effectively and to allow them sufficient time to learn. She identifies a link between the focus on speed of knowledge acquisition, which in the UK can be seen in the very young school starting ages and the prevalence of performativity in education, but also with the wider escalation of pace in society in relation to the use of technology and media, and, economically, in the increasing focus on efficiency of working time. The length of a typical day in a nursery is significantly longer than the three hours per day that is covered by early education funding in the UK and which is often the duration of nursery classes. There is an opportunity, then, for day nurseries to allow learning to be embedded in the flow of a more leisurely paced day, particularly in terms of mealtimes, care routines and time for sleep and relaxation. 'Time is money' is an oft-heard phrase, but time and child-paced practice as a precondition for high-quality childcare needs to be recognised and enabled.

6

Creating caring environments

Sociomateriality

Our relational understanding of the world, particularly for children, is inextricably linked to the material world, and increasingly the use of technology. Sociomateriality provides an insight into the influence of material objects, environments and technologies on children's and adults' learning and well-being, and recognises that human interaction, and early years practice, cannot be viewed in isolation from the material world. Sociomaterial considerations in nurseries include sleeping arrangements (cots, spread beds or the trend for 'coracle'-style beds), chairs, tables and other furnishings. Child-sized chairs in early childhood settings have been described as 'a contentious and ambiguous artefact' (Bone, 2019, p 134), and Maria Montessori asserted in 1912 that 'the principle of slavery still pervades pedagogy … I need only give one proof – the stationary desks and chairs' (1912, p 16). She noted that much attention was paid to children's ages and heights in determining the distance between seat and desk, but that the desks were constructed 'in such a way as to render the child visible in all his immobility' (Montessori, 1912, p 16). Similar concerns have been expressed about infants and toddlers being strapped into chairs (for their safety), as this constrains their movement and they have no autonomy or choice of seating position.

As the account of a baby's distress at a mealtime in Chapter 3 illustrated, practitioners can be challenged by conflicting demands at nursery mealtimes. Tara intervened to explain that the baby needed to feel settled and comfortable before he could be expected to be happy to sit in a highchair to eat, noting that the physical proximity (by allowing him to sit on her lap) would enable him to accept some food. The practitioner had been following 'normal' mealtime protocol and needed to be given the confidence to challenge and adapt the normal routine in order to cater for the child's emotional needs and, in turn, his nutritional requirements, and Tara's intervention helped to make her more aware of the impact of the physical restraint and separation that the highchair represented to the child.

The historic prevalence in nurseries of table-top activities, for which children need to be seated, has been gradually superseded by the use of fewer chairs, the growing popularity of stools, which take up less room, and the practice of encouraging children to stand at, and move freely between, activities that are placed on tables or other units. Many older toddlers and children feel more comfortable doing activities standing at tables or sitting on the floor. Rugs and cushions in book corners are often more inviting than children's chairs, and chairs are often only used in role-play areas by children who are pretending to be adults. Children are very tactile and express their feelings by the way they handle objects; as Sara Ahmed points out, 'emotions circulate through objects' (2004, p 194). Associations with objects affect both children and adults within early years settings. Practitioners also have to understand the emotional impact of physical objects and the way they're handled, taking account of individual children's backgrounds. This was noted by Helen, a manager of a nursery which had several vulnerable children in its care, some of whom struggled with sudden loud noises, such as doors slamming, because of previous traumatic experiences.

Other potentially fruitful aspects of materiality are the artifacts within childcare practice, including boundary objects, such as comforters, pacifiers, hygiene consumables, furnishings and toys. Technology is an increasingly important area of sociomateriality within childcare settings, and there is also a wider issue of nursery design, both within buildings and externally in outdoor play areas or entrances. The impact of material aspects of childcare settings is increasingly relevant to discussions of ethical practice, recognising that the skills and capabilities of practitioners are mediated by the capabilities of the tools and instruments being used (D'Adderio, 2021). The quality of childcare can be influenced by the nursery environment, from nursery design (Dudek, 2013) to the use of muted colours and soft furnishings in the communication-friendly spaces recommended by Elizabeth Jarman (2013). Some lighting can be harsh, and flexibility to allow soft lighting in some areas or at different times, such as sleep-time, can help to achieve calmer environments (Clare, 2012).

One example of sociomaterial impact on young children can be seen in Suzanne Zeedyk's research on the difference it makes when buggies are forwards- or backwards-facing (or, in her terminology, the latter being 'toward' the buggy pusher). Her data clearly show a strong correlation between the type of buggy and the amount of interaction, language and laughter of both parent and child, and she speculates that the higher number of infants and toddlers sleeping in 'toward'-facing buggies reflects their reduction in stress by being able to maintain visual contact and enjoy increased attentiveness from their carer. She suggests that the increasingly popular forwards-facing style of buggy may inadvertently be generating stress for infants. She says this is driven by changing cultural and technical demands (foldability to go into cars) as well as parents' underestimation of the importance of their emotional availability for their infants and toddlers and their assumption that very young children might benefit from looking out onto the world (Zeedyk, 2008). She suggests that simply turning the buggy around to face the pusher doubles the amount of conversation that babies experience, and a follow-up systematic observation by a nursery found that both children and staff report higher levels of enjoyment when out on a walk if they are facing each other (Zeedyk, 2014). Zeedyk's findings were foreshadowed by a psychiatrist in 1948, who observed that with 'the introduction of the perambulator the need for adequate body contact is often forgotten' (Montagu, 1986, p 96).

The sociomateriality of mobile phones, tablets and screens is ubiquitous in modern family life, and in nurseries there is increasing use of apps and online record-keeping, particularly taking photos and making observations to share with parents. Toddlers are adept at using anything vaguely rectangular as imitation phones through which to chat to imaginary family members, and we noticed a dramatic increase in the familiarity of even very young children with the technology of phones after the COVID-19 lockdown. In many ways, nurseries offer a welcome respite from screen time and hopefully help to support parents and carers to realise that phones can interfere with direct communication. As Paula, a nursery practitioner, described, ground rules may need to be set:

> In my previous setting, parents used to come … and pick their children up, on their phone, and there would be no interaction at all … it just became upsetting for us and for the child. It was no, like, how was your day? They'd just literally take them and take them out to their car.

Practitioner well-being

Soft furnishings and comfortable seating are not just a consideration for the children in a nursery. Material objects can affect the quality of care practices. For childcare practitioners to provide caregiving in a way that is emotionally and physically rewarding, it is important that they are comfortable. Few of the interviewees mentioned their physical comfort or discomfort within their caring roles, which is not surprising, as the provision, or not, of comfortable seating for infant feeding, for example, may not be questioned if a practitioner has not experienced differences in nurseries in terms of having comfortable chairs in baby rooms. Liz, a trainer and consultant who had visited a wide range of settings in her work, commented on the difference between nurseries where practitioners have had to improvise with cushions on the floor and those where they have comfortable chairs. Her assertion that it 'has an impact then on the attachment' is borne out by the neuroscience research on the importance of babies being 'lovingly held' (Gerhardt, 2004, p 40). On being asked to describe her perfect nursery, Liz described a nurturing feel and said that it 'had, like, sofas'.

When Amber, a senior practitioner, described how to bottle-feed a baby, she advised: 'Make sure you're comfortable and make sure the baby's comfortable.' She used the phrases 'sit on you comfortably' and 'give as much comfort', indicating the importance of physical ease within the feeding routine, both for practitioners and infants. I have noticed that nurseries where there is a clear focus on nurturing care also have comfortable seating for infant feeding – for practitioners, but also for visiting breastfeeding mothers. Conversely, the impression I have gained from other nurseries is that there is a reluctance to provide seating that might encourage practitioners to be *too* relaxed, which may reflect the level of trust in practitioner conduct and whether the management of the nursery adopted a Theory X or Theory Y perspective of their staff teams (McGregor, 2006). Theory X is based on negative assumptions about an employee's motivation and attitude. Rules and supervision are seen as important to ensure efficient working. A manager with this perspective would worry that sofas encourage sitting, perhaps assuming that practitioners should be continually active. Conversely, Theory Y managers would trust their team members to use a sofa appropriately, for times when cuddles, storytelling or feeding might be enhanced by more comfortable seating.

Regardless of whether comfortable seating is provided, baby room practices depend on the situational context – the social interactions with colleagues and the time constraints for one-to-one care practices. Mandatory staffing ratios within baby rooms in the UK are one staff member to three infants or toddlers under two years of age. There is, therefore, additional pressure on other colleagues if a practitioner lingers with one child – for example, on a bottle feed. Balancing the needs of individual children against the needs of the whole group is a daily practice of sensemaking on the part of practitioners, and I explore this in the next chapter.

The well-being of early years professionals is not wholly dependent on the quality of staff room facilities, but there is no doubt that having a comfortable and attractive room to take a break in is an important feature of a nursery that cares about its staff team. Having facilities that encourage early years professionals to take breaks with colleagues also encourages team togetherness and mutual support, and restricting conversations within the playrooms to professional dialogue is much easier if a time and a place is provided for team members to have a rest, refreshments and a chance to discuss personal issues or last night's television viewing. At Acorn, we once took over a nursery that had been refurbished in all the areas that parents might see, but had a very dilapidated staff room. Making that room a more comfortable and professional space was an easy win to make the team feel valued and lift morale. Similarly, providing chilled and filtered water and personalised water bottles has proved to be an effective 'carrot' to encourage practitioners to adopt healthy drinking habits in the workplace while at the same time role-modelling this behaviour to children.

At a more basic level, there is also the need to ensure that adults working in a setting can comfortably spend time at a child's level. Not everyone is comfortable sitting on a child's chair, so the provision of low adult chairs is important. Similarly, if we expect our practitioners to spend time outdoors with the children, an ethic of care would suggest that provision of warm outdoor clothing would help staff facilitate outdoor play and learning with children comfortably and help to ensure that adults are able to role-model enthusiasm for being outdoors all year round. If practitioners are expected to wear a uniform, it is also important to consider comfort in the selection of items. Unisex items are often too boxy, so at Acorn we have different styles of polo shirts, for example, to suit all body shapes. Two of my interviewees complained about the impracticality of the stipulation at a nursery they had both worked at previously that practitioners should wear tailored skirts of a certain length. Peta noted that the uniform made her look as if she worked in a bank, and Kim described rebelling against the skirt rule, as it was particularly impractical in the baby room, where she was working. Items related to health and safety, such as aprons and plastic gloves, are commonly provided, but even these are not without ethical issues.

Problematic protective clothing and equipment and outdoor clothing

Protective clothing in nurseries is usually limited to aprons and gloves for care practices, mealtimes and messy play. During the COVID-19 pandemic, the issue of personal protective equipment (PPE), or rather the lack of it, became a major focus for safety. Protective single-use gloves and aprons also have ethical implications in terms of sustainability. Restricting the use of PPE to save money is an unethical practice if it has a negative impact on practitioner safety and well-being, but another reason for minimising the use of disposable PPE is the environmental factor. Sharon, a director at a large nursery chain, was keen to ban the use of single-use plastic in her nurseries for this reason, but felt she had to compromise to keep staff satisfied their needs were being met: 'I don't want to lose a member of staff over plastic gloves. You know, if she's great and, or he is great in every other way, then the compromise I will make will be to say use one plastic glove.' She ascribed the reluctance to abandon gloves to prior training, referring to 'nurseries where the manager or baby room manager is ex-NNEB [holds the National Nursery Examination Board qualification] and would not move to not using gloves'. The reference to this old qualification suggests that those refusing to comply with the sustainable practice tended to be more mature practitioners with more experience and confidence to object to practices they don't agree with.

There is another problem with PPE, unrelated to cost and environmental impact, and that is the potential impact on children. The example of plastic gloves being worn when applying suncream, as described in the previous chapter, prompted a debate about whether it is right or wrong to use gloves when wiping the noses of children too young to do it themselves, and the reflections that ensued were about how that might feel for children – parents almost certainly wouldn't use gloves for that task at home, so the children might be disconcerted by a practitioner's unwillingness to do this without being gloved up. This echoes the experience of practical learning involving cold and warm flannels described in Chapter 2 and is an example of 'the materiality of organizational experience that often evades analytical-rational description and which stems from the knowledge-evoking process' (Strati, 2007, p 65), which in this case involves increased awareness of the impact of the simple caring action of wiping clean a child's face.

Protective clothing for children can also be a factor in whether childcare is inclusive. The issue is not necessarily the clothing itself, but its availability. The kind of clothing I mean is the provision of warm outdoor coats, boots, gloves and hats, particularly wet weather clothing or clothing that protects a child's normal clothes from being soiled in messy activities. A child who lacks sufficient warm layers and protection from wet weather will be unable to enjoy outdoor activities. That is an easily recognised problem which is often addressed with a nursery stock of spares. It is an example of Tronto's (1993; 2013) 'caring about' whether a child has appropriate clothing in order to feel comfortable and 'taking care of' the child by assuming responsibility for providing that clothing if the parent or carer has forgotten or is unable to supply it.

What is sometimes missed, however, is the impact of children going home with wet or dirty clothes, particularly coats. Not every family will have easy access to washing and drying facilities, and not every family will have a spare coat for their child to wear while their usual coat is being cleaned. Clothes being damaged in any way or going missing can be distressing for a family on a tight budget. Similarly, a casual comment about a child's boots being too small, with a request for a new pair to be provided, can unwittingly cause further stress and upset. This extends *caring about* to the wider family. Developing a good stock of outdoor wear for any child to use is a facilitator of stress-free play for the child and may be a welcome relief for parents and carers. Also, protecting a child's indoor clothes with effective aprons may prevent a tense exchange with family members at the end of the day.

Finally, footwear and clothing can unwittingly inhibit children from engaging in a full range of play experiences and may also reinforce gender stereotypes. Too often, girls' clothes and shoes are designed around how they look rather than their practicality, and the messaging of 'little princess' and 'superhero' on clothes will send a clear signal to children of gendered expectations. Providing unisex warm and waterproof outdoor clothing for children to wear can help to counter this subliminal gendering and ensure that all children have access to the full range of outdoor experiences, regardless of their parents' ability to provide appropriate clothing.

Play equipment

The quality of equipment and resources used by children can also have ethical consequences, as in the story of the left-handed child struggling with right-handed scissors in Vignette 6.1. That case reflects an apparent failing on the practitioner's part, as left-handed scissors were clearly readily available in the setting but had not been identified by the practitioner as being needed by this child. Similarly, there have been many accounts of children of colour not being given an appropriate palette of colours when being asked to do self-portraits. This is despite it being very easy to ensure diversity of resources in books, role play areas and small world resources.

Vignette 6.1: The wrong scissors

Clare, an early years consultant, described her observation of 'an adult-directed activity with some scissors' with a practitioner who was herself observing and making notes about four children who were cutting along prescribed lines. After the activity, Clare asked the practitioner how she felt the activity had gone, and her response was that she was impressed with the three girls' ability to cut the paper along the lines. On enquiring about the other child, the response was that he 'can't use a pair of scissors'. Clare noted that the child was in earshot at this point and she commented that this made her 'really upset'.

Clare recounted how she then modelled a more successful supportive role to the practitioner, explaining afterwards that she had provided the correct scissors: 'The biggest mistake that you have made today is ... you have just given a left-handed child right-handed scissors. That child was failing from the beginning. And you need to be mindful of that.' The child had been excluded at the point when the practitioner failed to recognise their need for left-handed scissors.

A question that arises from the scissors incident is whether the practitioner was aware of the difference between the pairs of scissors (left-handed and right-handed scissors usually have different-coloured handles to differentiate between them), and if not, whether that was due to inadequate training, induction or leadership within the room. It is highly unlikely that it would have been in any way deliberate, but it is not possible now to ascertain the reason for the lack of reflection and problem-solving. It is possible that gender stereotyping may have played a part – boys are often perceived as having less patience and interest in fine motor skills than girls, so the boy's struggles may have been unconsciously ascribed to his gender rather than his left-handedness.

The type of toys and equipment in a nursery often reflects the depth of knowledge of owners or managers – whether they are aware of current best practice and the impact of sociomateriality. There is certainly more awareness now of the impact of boundary objects and pacifiers (Van Laere et al, 2019). Use of take-home teddies, for example, have been questioned. This is a popular practice of encouraging children to take home the nursery teddy and then bring in photos of what the teddy did. The impact of this practice on social inclusivity was highlighted in a discussion among a group of nursery managers at an Acorn meeting. An area manager asked managers how they felt personally about similar practices in schools, and one opened up about how much she dreaded her nephew's turn with the school bear, as she was providing kinship care for him and was keen to maintain privacy around his family's difficult circumstances. Other managers then commented on how competitive the teddy's holidays became, with some parents in more affluent nurseries seeming keen to impress. The discussion led to a blog post to draw attention to the implications of a well-meaning but potentially problematic practice. An ethic of care, in its focus on the impact on individuals, may help to question such practices.

The use of colour and different materials in the decor of a nursery can also have a significant impact on the feel of the place. Looking back on photographs taken at one of our nurseries in the early 1990s, I am struck by the bold use of colour and the murals painted on a wall, not to mention some very bright plastic toys that would now look very out of place. Maya, a nursery manager, described the noticeable impact on a child's behaviour and well-being of a nursery that had been decorated with very bold primary colours. One child became very upset every time she was taken into the yellow room, but calmed down in every other room. Maya asserted: 'I will never forget that for as long as I live.' She described how she tried to persuade the director to redecorate in more neutral colours, but this couldn't be done because 'it was all about cost', so she had to move the child into the next age group to solve the problem.

There is a very welcome increase in the use of natural resources, loose parts and 'real' artefacts in many nurseries. The key to these resources being successful, as with a range of toys, is skilful deployment by practitioners. Liz, a consultant who had been engaged by the owner of a nursery to support a new manager, described what she found:

It was under-resourced, that was the first thing, and it was, it was a mess as well. Now that doesn't mean that a mess is a bad thing, because children create that kind of, don't they? But there's a mess and there's a mess, if you know what I mean … it was unpurposeful mess, and it was under-resourced, and the staff were very kind of disengaged.

I had often observed the same distinction in nursery environments, where it is often very clear whether a busy, messy range of activities in a nursery is attractive and engaging to children or simply adding clutter and lacking purpose. Resources that are in poor condition, not looked after and not well presented are far less likely to engage a child than a curated collection of invitations to play. Amy, a deputy manager, described the 'Duplo drop' practice at a nursery where she worked previously as a practitioner, which relied on simply providing different toys to play with, and another practitioner, Emily, said that her previous nursery wouldn't allow messy activities and described what happened when big red boxes of plastic toys were placed on the table:

And then if, obviously, if a child sees a box, it's full of toys, what they're going to do? They're going to tip it up. So, you know, straight away they tipped it up, on the floor, and then they would get told off! For tipping up the box. So, yeah, things like that. It wasn't right … it upset me actually, working there.

Another advantage of loose parts and natural resources is that they support non-gendered play. As illustrated by the word clouds in Figure 6.1 from the inspiring Let Toys Be Toys campaign, although there has been progress in recent years, toy advertising consistently reinforces stereotypical views of what children are attracted by, which inevitably influences their toy choices. Non-gendered play equipment is essential in nurseries, and we shouldn't underestimate the scale of the task facing us if we are to achieve gender equity. Before leaving the topic of play equipment, I'd like to stress the importance of adult encouragement and facilitation in the play process. The benefits of play do not depend on the quality of the resources and play equipment as much as the way in which play opportunities are curated. In order for children to develop skills in self-regulation, they need adults who are attuned to them and who can help them navigate the world of play (Conkbayir, 2023). This means structuring the environment appropriately for children who may need to be able to retreat to a calm and quiet space. This is about decor and furnishings rather than play equipment, and it depends on early years professionals facilitating child-led learning and play with resources that can adapt to the needs of children to support them to express themselves and develop their communication and cooperation skills. We need to take play seriously. As one inspirational advocate of play explains: 'Play is therapeutic discipline with a unique capacity to heal emotional damage through positive biochemistry' (Kingston-Hughes, 2022, p 3).

Figure 6.1: TV toy advertising: for boys and girls

Source: Let Toys Be Toys (2021)

The outdoors as the third pedagogue

Margaret McMillan, a pioneer of nursery schools in England (see Chapter 4), created an open air nursery in Deptford in East London over 100 years ago. A quote attributed to McMillan is still relevant: 'the best classroom and the richest cupboard is roofed only by the sky'. In *The Nursery School*, she paints a vivid picture of a nursery garden planted with trees, fruit and vegetables: 'The children love the herbs. The toddlers press their leaves with their little fingers, and come into the shelter smelling their hands. The three-year-olds do the same' (McMillan, 1919, p 46). She also describes the need for an uncultivated space: 'a Nursery garden must have a free and rich place, a great rubbish heap, stones, flints, bits of can, and old iron and pots. Here every healthy child will want to go; taking out things of his own choosing to build with' (McMillan, 1919, p 47).

In a section which should feel like a historical account, but unfortunately will resonate with practitioners working in some deprived urban areas today, there is also a very poignant and disturbing description of the impact of the school's closure period in August each year, when the children would be confined in unsanitary and cramped living conditions: 'Charlie will go back into a grim room at the back of a grim shop in a grim back street. There will be no more play under the great planes and mulberry where the leaf shadows fall on scores of little heads' (McMillan, 1919, p 305). McMillan notes that on their return in September, about 20 per cent of the children were suffering from skin and eye diseases. She describes cases of children's physical and psychological health being dramatically improved as well as 'greatly increased responsiveness and intelligence' from attending the open-air nursery school daily (McMillan, 1919, p 329). At the end of her book, she praises the 1918 bill that 'sets forth that Nursery-Schools, preferably open-air, shall be opened for little children' (McMillan, 1919, p 350) and describes the impact of this:

> All the neglected, suffering, dirty little children now playing in the gutter, and near roaring traffic and hooting cars will be gathered into gardens at last. And what can this mean? A garden-grown humanity cannot be as the humanity of the grime and of the street. It will have spent its first cycle in a place where living things are taken care of so that at least they spring up into things of beauty, and colour, and perfume. Those who do all this culture work will be cultured. The little gardeners themselves, not the flowers or the vegetables or the trees, will be the glory of the garden. (McMillan, 1919, p 351)

The recognition of the importance of outdoor play and learning for children perhaps diminished after this promising start over 100 years ago, but interest has increased in recent years. In some countries, of course, this has been embedded in early years practice for many years. In the Nordic countries, children in early care and education settings spend a large part of their day outdoors, and nature is considered an important place for play and learning. In Norway, a public report stated that children should not play indoors for more than two hours at a time (Sandseter and Lysklett, 2017, p 119).

Large, deep sandboxes, which originated in Denmark (Jensen, 2011), or sandpits as they are more commonly known in the UK, are seen by both children and early years professionals as important features in the outdoor areas of early childhood settings, and their value is usually recognised by families too. Occasionally, however, parents need to have the benefits of sand play explained to them. Acorn took over a nursery which had a large sunken sandpit that had been fenced off and empty for some time. We reinstated it, filling it with sand, to the delight of the children, and most parents were pleased to see the improvement in the outdoor facilities, though one expressed concern – because it meant their child might go home with sand in their clothes and because they felt a sandpit had nothing educational to offer! Perhaps my confidence that there has been a general movement away from narrow perceptions of early learning is misplaced. There was certainly a depressing trend for several years towards the use of universal soft surfaces and artificial grass, but there is increasing recognition now of the importance of natural resources, and few nurseries today do not have a bug hotel and a mud kitchen as part of their outdoor environment.

The ethic of care has a crucial role in outdoor play and learning, particularly in embedding sustainability into early years settings. Children have an innate curiosity which can be encouraged and rewarded in the richness of a natural environment. An area of soil, with its bugs and worms, a variety of plants, particularly those which attract bees and butterflies, and ideally space to grow plants and trees that bear fruit can provide an ideal environment for children to explore and discover living creatures and plants that need nurturing. For children to develop a caring attitude towards nature, they need to experience it first-hand. As the author who named the concept of nature deficit disorder observed: 'We cannot protect something we do not love, we cannot love what we do not know, and we cannot know what we do not see. Or hear. Or sense' (Louv, 2012, p 104). Caroline Lucas of the Green Party identifies as a problem 'our tendency to treat nature as something beautiful yet separate' (2024, p 156). Early years settings are ideally placed to encourage children's fascination with the living world, and there are proven benefits to children of handling soil (Scudellari, 2017).

Caring for plants and animals provides easily understood opportunities for children to learn about how to care for others, but outdoor play and learning often offers a multitude of opportunities to assist others and develop collaborative skills, such as when helping another child to climb a muddy bank, build a den or find minibeasts to examine. Even urban environments can offer green spaces and locations for litter-picking activities. With the appropriate equipment and guidance, children can safely achieve a noticeable improvement to an area, take satisfaction in their achievement and gain an understanding of the consequences of throwing litter on the ground. Being outdoors also offers benefits such as providing a less confined space, which can help children to self-regulate and relax, as well as offering physical benefits of fresh air, vitamin D from sunlight and farther horizons, which are important for children's eye health. Forest school sessions in particular offer children opportunities for collaborative activities and more autonomy, helping to boost their confidence and self-esteem.

7

Ethical sensemaking and how individuals can make a difference

The process of sensemaking and sensegiving

In exploring the influences on ethical practice and how to implement an ethic of care, intentionality and ethical decision-making are clearly important factors, and these lead to a consideration of sensemaking, particularly when using practice theory. Sensemaking is 'the process through which people work to understand issues or events that are novel, ambiguous, confusing, or in some other way violate expectations' (Maitlis and Christianson, 2014, p 57) and an activity that can 'capture the lived experience of organising' (Maitlis et al, 2013, p 240). As a theoretical concept, it can help in analysing how ethical intentions affect practices in early years provision. It is particularly useful for examining social processes, including those that are affected by power and emotions, and the embodied and sociomaterial nature of practices, all of which are key in early years practice. Sensemaking is a perspective, or a set of heuristics, rather than a single theory (Weick, 1995; Sandberg and Tsoukas, 2015), and it has some features in common with reflective practice, a familiar concept to early years professionals. Sensemaking can be applied both to individuals and to organisational cultures and behaviours, and its corollary, sensegiving, is an important aspect of relational leadership. I am particularly interested in the way ethical behaviours are facilitated or hindered, so the kind of sensemaking I applied in my research analysis was ethical sensemaking, but before discussing that, I will explain how sensemaking has developed as a concept.

Karl Weick is widely regarded as one of the first key scholars of sensemaking, but as he acknowledged himself, the concept has its roots with the philosophers and psychologists William James, George Herbert Mead (who was also a sociologist) and John Dewey (who was also an educationalist). Their pragmatist approach focused attention on social processes as a way of understanding the world, using a social constructionist approach which has been developed by many writers across different disciplines. Weick insisted on the retrospective character of sensemaking, and he viewed it as an inherently social action, not synonymous with interpretation, but rather using interpretation as a component (Weick, 1995; 2012).

He saw language, rather than cognition, as the locus of sensemaking, and he recognised the importance and impact of stories within organisations. His suggestion that sensemaking should be of particular concern to organisations which are more 'open' and influenced by environmental factors makes its application within early years settings highly appropriate given the ways in which childcare settings have to adapt to changing levels of funding, market conditions, regulations and economic conditions. Settings are also influenced by political, social and emotional factors, and practitioners have to tailor their practice to deal with a wide range of families. Sensemaking is, therefore, a continual process for many adults within childcare settings, as they seek to understand the appropriate response to situations which can change rapidly and dramatically from day to day and even over the course of a single day.

Different typologies of sensemaking have been developed, and there is ongoing debate about what triggers or initiates sensemaking. Sally Maitlis identifies distinct forms of organisational sensemaking according to the level of sensegiving taking place, whether by leaders or stakeholders; sensegiving is taken to mean the process of attempting to influence sensemaking towards an organisation's preferred interpretation of a situation, and it is seen as 'a fundamental leadership activity within organizational sensemaking' (Maitlis, 2005, p 22). She concludes that high levels of sensegiving by leaders or stakeholders lead to 'guided organizational sensemaking' with high levels of animation and control, and an emergent series of actions that is internally consistent (Maitlis, 2005). She draws further conclusions about the fragmentation of sensemaking in situations where leaders, stakeholders or both have low levels of sensegiving. I use her model of organisational sensemaking in Figure 7.1 to illustrate how this might be applied to early years settings.

Sandberg and Tsoukas (2020) put forward another typology of sensemaking, based on the difference between the purpose of the sensemaking process and its core constituents. I use this in Table 7.1 to help in understanding the sensemaking that takes place within early years settings and the link with reflective practice. Their 'absorbed coping' type of sensemaking, for example, resonates with the concept of 'reflection-in-action' (Schon, 1983), which focuses on tacit, instinctive knowledge and skills. Reflection-on-action is comparable to the deliberate types of sensemaking.

As shown in Table 7.1, Sandberg and Tsoukas' (2020) first type is *immanent* sensemaking, which is described as absorbed coping. This refers to the kind of routine activities which require minimal cognitive-discursive sensing, and the responses that might be considered subconscious and instinctive by experienced practitioners or agents. This, I feel, is a helpful way to frame the kind of sensemaking that takes place when practitioners are working out how to deal with distressed toddlers, for example. There is

Figure 7.1: Ethical sensegiving model, based on a model of organisational sensemaking

	Low ethical awareness and sensegiving from practitioner	High ethical awareness and sensegiving from practitioner
High ethical commitment and sensegiving from leader/organisation	**Restricted ethical sensemaking** Policies in place but not consistently practiced or embedded – risk of ethical slippage	**Embedded ethical sensemaking** Policies and internally consistent practice – an embedded ethic of care
Low ethical sensegiving from leader/ organisation	**Minimal ethical sensemaking** Carewashing in policies and likelihood of poor practice becoming embedded	**Fragmented ethical sensemaking** Pockets of ethical practice that are not consistent and not supported by organisational culture

Sensegiving →

Source: Based on Maitlis (2005, p 32)

no rule book to follow – it is more of a reliance on embodied skills and intuition as well as the tacit knowledge that is an important aspect of reflection-in-action (Schon, 1983). Their second type, *involved-deliberate* sensemaking, refers to a more conscious and probably more discursive practice, where practitioners might debate the correct course of action – for example, referral of a child's minor injury or ill health to parents or health professionals, or reflection-*on*-action, which may include conscious consideration of how care practices are being received by a child. The latter may be part of absorbed coping, but occurs afterwards, taking it into involved-deliberate sensemaking. Sandberg and Tsoukas's third form of sensemaking is *detached-deliberate*, and this would apply to retrospective debate about problematic situations and to interpretations of external policies and guidance – the kind that took place in nurseries during the COVID-19 pandemic, for example. Finally, the authors' *representational* sensemaking takes the detachment a step further and applies to the kinds of situation that involve external parties – investigations of accidents or complaints, for example.

Thus, as illustrated in Table 7.1, sensemaking takes place at a variety of levels, from the unconscious, embodied level of care routines to a more deliberately conscious level of sensemaking. A nursery manager recounted an example where a practitioner became concerned during a nappy change

Table 7.1: Typology of sensemaking in early years settings

Features of sensemaking	Types of sensemaking			
	Immanent	Involved-deliberate	Detached-deliberate	Representational
Location of sensemaking	Primary practice world – within childcare settings			Secondary practice world – external discussions about policies and practice
Ontological category	Absorbed coping – day-to-day childcare practices, adapting to children's individual needs; reflection-in-action; awareness of power relations during care practices	Involved thematic deliberation – becoming conscious of methods being used; challenges to assumptions	Abstract detachment – reflections on practice (reflection-on-action)	Theoretical detachment – discussions about childcare practice; not specific to a setting
Object of sensemaking	Routine childcare activities (for example, adapting sleep routines for each child or noticing a change in a child's demeanour); conscious awareness of how care is being received	Interrupted activities or challenges to the way activities are undertaken (for example, a nursery manager or senior practitioner noticing and correcting poor practice and explaining their rationale)	Problematic/problematised activities – discussion or reflection about practice or events (for example, a professional discussion between colleagues about changes needed in response to external events)	Problematic/problematised decontextualised activities – challenges within childcare practices in general (for example, discussions with parents about requests which breach nursery policies, perhaps by reinforcing gendered role-play)
Purpose for organisation	Enacting routine activities – ensuring consistent quality	Restoring interrupted activities–resolving differences in practice	Reviewing problematic/problematised activities – also reviewing incidents or complaints	Explaining problematic/problematised activities – to understand how childcare should be practised
Specific sense generated	Practical sense – how individuals in a setting conceive of practice	Contextual sense – how teams within a setting conceive of practice	Conceptual sense – how organisations conceive of practice	Spectatorial sense – external advisory view of practice by academic and other experts

Table 7.1: Typology of sensemaking in early years settings (continued)

Features of sensemaking	Types of sensemaking			
	Immanent	Involved-deliberate	Detached-deliberate	Representational
Core constituents				
Sense–action nexus	Unified	Partly unified, partly separate	Temporarily separate	Completely separate
Temporality	Practical (immediate-anticipatory); existential – in-the-moment planning and adapting routines and personal care practices	Practical (immediate); pragmatically chronological (retrospective-prospective) – in the moment, but may have an impact on future practice	Pragmatically chronological (retrospective-prospective) – reviewing actions and practices after events or incidents	Analytically chronological (retrospective-prospective) – discussing and rationalising past actions to explain or to adapt policies moving forward
Embodiment	Principally bodily; minimally cognitive-discursive sensing – instinctively adapting how to settle a child to sleep; conscious awareness of impact of care practice on a child	Partly bodily; partly cognitive-discursive sensing – instinctive reaction to comfort a child; challenging the 'normal' mealtime protocol of children remaining seated	Little bodily; mainly cognitive-discursive sensing – professional discussion about the correct course of action following an incident or accident	Minimally bodily; principally cognitive-discursive sensing – discussions with parents about policies and practices in the nursery

Source: Based on Sandberg and Tsoukas (2020, p 9)

by the breathing of one of the babies, which seemed to her to be laboured in that the baby's chest was rising more than usual with each breath. She discussed her concerns with colleagues, some of whom did not share her conviction that there was a problem. The parents of the child did not consider it to be a problem either. But she trusted her intuition that the child's breathing was atypical and a cause for concern, and this was borne out when the child was subsequently admitted to hospital after paramedics were called. Having confidence in personal intuition and observations was critical in this case, as it can be when dealing with safeguarding concerns, where an intuition that something doesn't seem right needs to be taken seriously and acted on.

Sensegiving, as shown in Figure 7.1, is an important aspect of sensemaking. It was originally used to describe the way a leader might disseminate a vision of strategic change to an organisation's stakeholders (Gioia and Chittipeddi, 1991). Within the context of the early years sector and ethical childcare practice, the term can usefully be applied to the way in which nursery leaders and senior practitioners might influence the sensemaking of others towards a preferred understanding of best practice, and this might involve other colleagues, parents and external trainers and consultants. It is concerned with influencing the interpretations of others and has therefore been described as 'a political activity' (Maitlis and Lawrence, 2007, p 77). Inclusivity, the prioritisation of a child's needs above the organisational drivers for efficiency or profit, and the attentiveness and time required for ethical, respectful care practices can be challenging for early years providers, as illustrated in my research interviews with a wide range of leaders and practitioners. Where practitioners have felt a disconnect with their personal moral code, they sometimes engaged in sensegiving themselves. Nursery manager Kim described overruling practitioners who were trying to force a child with additional needs to sit at a table. She reminded them that she was the special educational needs coordinator (SENCO) and said: 'No, if he wants to go and play, he can go and play, and they, you could see it not computing in their heads.' She also described how she developed the understanding and practice of the two other team members in the room over the next six months, an extended piece of sensegiving as it allowed them to understand the rationale behind her apparent disregard for normal practice.

Sensegiving as values articulation

The act of sensegiving has commonalities with the articulation of a setting's values. Explicitly articulating a moral purpose can help to focus awareness of it and create a value commitment and reference point within an organisation. 'Values work' (Gehman et al, 2013) recognises that practices are inevitably suffused with values, and my research interviews highlighted several instances where managers or senior practitioners explained the rationale behind actions as a form of sensegiving which also embedded a nursery's values and ethos. An example provided by a nursery manager is provided in Vignette 7.1.

Vignette 7.1: Kieran's induction for a new member of staff

A nursery manager, Cara, described an example of sensegiving in action involving Kieran, an experienced member of staff, and Emma, a new member of staff. Kieran explained to Emma how another experienced colleague was sensitively supporting a child who was struggling to regulate her emotions. Kieran articulated the rationale behind his colleague's response to the child, which was infused with the respectful care ethos of the nursery. In Cara's words:

Kieran runs the garden induction. It's very practical. You're with him in the garden for a few hours. He's talking you through what he sees, and that is an invaluable thing. You know, some people in early years can look and they can see. But most people look and they don't know what they're looking at. So what I do is mentor them up with people who really know what they're looking at. And then I ask them just to stand with them and then just to listen to what that person is seeing, and I know that it's high quality, I know that they're able to showcase things.

So the other day in the garden, a little girl was very upset. She was crying and something had not gone her way. There was nothing major. She just wasn't regulating her emotions in that moment. So Kieran was explaining to … Emma what was going on. He watched as Sonia went over to the child. She came down to her level, she said: 'Would you like a cuddle. I'm here for you.' And the child shouted in her face 'No I'm not. I don't want a cuddle', and she pushed her away. So Sonia just moved away from the child and sat down on the floor. She just gave a very open body language and she said: 'I am here whenever you need me.' The child wasn't able in that moment to accept that support. But after a few minutes she sidestepped, sidestepped, sidestepped, gradually sat down, and Sonia very gently just put her arm around her. And just gave her the right level of support at the right time. And Kieran was able to articulate that to a new member of staff to showcase how this competent practitioner was supporting the child, without taking over or stealing the learning away from the experience. And so that's really a crucial skill which is far greater than a manager can offer – it's practice on the floor.

The example in Vignette 7.1 may read like a typical form of coaching, but Cara was keen to explain how she and her colleagues used every opportunity to instil their respectful care ethos, and articulating the rationale behind a course of action is a type of sensegiving. Without this sensegiving, an inexperienced practitioner may misinterpret an instruction to offer comfort to an upset child or make assumptions about how and why this should be done. So while there is overlap between coaching and sensegiving, ethical sensegiving is about communicating underlying ethical principles. The earlier example of Kim overruling practitioners who had unrealistic expectations of a child with additional needs illustrates an ethics-driven piece of sensegiving that was delivered in stages. Without her articulation of why their practice was not in the child's best interests, there was a risk that her instructions would only be followed when she was there to witness it. Sensegiving has an important role in organisational learning, but the critical point is that it always has a practical context; it is 'involved-deliberate' if delivered at the time, or 'detached-deliberate' if reflecting back on an example of practice (following Sandberg and Tsoukas, 2020).

The example in Vignette 7.1 demonstrates how a respectful care ethos can give rise to values articulation, but implementing an ethic of care applies not just to pedagogy and care practice but also to the way in which the organisation is led and managed. In Chapter 3, I noted that John, chief executive of a large organisation, described maintaining 'a moral compass' as one of the most important but most challenging aspects of his role. Having a moral compass, like having a personal ethic of care, is not necessarily going to encourage others to follow suit, so values articulation is one way in which leaders and managers can relate decisions to an underpinning ethos as a guiding principle. In the early years sector, that needs to include the way employees are treated as well as how children's families are treated.

Ethical sensemaking and decision-making

Sensemaking is often equated with decision-making in the face of a crisis or in the aftermath of an incident or disaster, when the causes need to be identified in order to prevent a future occurrence. In the context of early years practice, such sensemaking is thankfully rarely needed, but when it is, it often exposes the inadequacy of relying on policies, which have limitations in unforeseen circumstances. As I am particularly concerned with ethical sensemaking, the situations of particular interest are those where decisions have unethical consequences. Ethical sensemaking focuses on situations where the consequences of an action or decision may have unintentionally unethical consequences, in particular where the 'right' thing to do is not immediately obvious. It also applies to reflections on practice when engaged in the 'care-receiving' phase of care (Tronto, 1993; 2013), when trying to ascertain whether an action or care practice achieved its intended outcome and when heightening awareness of power relations.

Ethical decision-making may be deliberated between colleagues or at government or local authority levels of policy making, but it can also be intuitive and non-deliberate. The extent of individual agency and autonomy within early years settings influences decision-making processes, and ethical sensemaking may be triggered by conflicts about how policies should be interpreted and implemented. Early years professionals may directly challenge and openly disagree with policies or practices they deem unethical, but their actions can often be more accurately described as instances of 'micro resistance', which may be 'local, quiet, invisible and multiple' (Archer, 2021, p 9). Examples from my interviews included allowing children to access activities or meals that should have been subject to additional charges and allowing messier and riskier play than was approved by a nursery's management.

The level of resistance often reflected the level of seniority of decision makers. One nursery manager, Tara, recounted an example at her previous nursery:

> The two-year funding, we weren't allowed to take … with the special educational needs we were told 'no, you're not allowed to take them',

but we took them anyway, because for me, that's — you can't just exclude a child just because they've got Downs syndrome or because they've got severe autism.

Tara's personal care ethic enabled her to challenge unethical practice, and her confidence was bolstered by knowing that her ethical instincts were aligned to the guidance from Ofsted and the local authority, so the owner of the organisation she worked in would have no grounds for an official sanction. She said that the owner's rationale was 'it was too much paperwork involved, too much time involved', and continued: 'We took the children anyway, but we, we got a lot of stick for it.'

Ethical sensemaking can also take place with and by children. On my Icelandic study tour, mentioned in Chapter 2, the most memorable activity for me was when a group of children out on a nature walk discovered a dead bird. There was a discussion (translated for us by the pedagogues) about what might have caused the small bird's death, and one of the children pointed out a cat that was prowling at a short distance. She was very concerned that the cat might take the bird and expressed a desire to take the bird back to the nursery to give it a burial. The gist of the pedagogue's response was that she shouldn't handle the dead bird with bare hands, but that if she could find something to transport it on, it would be fine to take it back. A search by some of the children discovered a piece of tarpaulin, which then became a makeshift bier, held by four children on a procession back to the nursery. We then observed at a respectful distance the children's organisation of a burial and a simple ceremony, which felt poignant, caring and solemn, but not at all gloomy. The impression I had was that the children were proud of creating a proper resting place for the little bird, who had also been subjected to a close examination prior to burial, with a pedagogue using the opportunity to show and describe the bird's features to the small group of budding biologists.

The ethical sensemaking in this episode was undertaken by the pedagogues, who had to decide how to respond to the child's concern for the dead bird. In taking seriously her concern about the threat of the cat, they demonstrated a respect and care for her feelings and used the opportunity to give the children a problem-solving exercise, explaining why they shouldn't touch dead animals, but allowing them to find a practical solution and then providing further learning opportunities back at the nursery about the bird's anatomy and what would happen to its body after burial. The impromptu introduction to the subject of death was also a sensemaking experience for the children in debating the 'right' thing to do with the dead bird and collectively planning and implementing an appropriate ceremony. I would have liked to have understood the intense discussion taking place between the children during the challenging task of agreeing what song to sing over the bird's grave, but once they had reached a consensus and completed the simple ceremony, there was no mistaking their pride and satisfaction. As with the risky play witnessed on the same trip (see Chapter 2), I was struck by the confidence and autonomy of both the pedagogues and the children, and I wondered whether the same resolution could have been achieved in an English nursery without someone questioning whether it would be 'allowed'.

Ethical decision-making and sensemaking in nurseries is occasionally complicated by conflicting loyalties and sometimes by a dissonance within an individual's personal morality. In some cases, interviewees were very forthright about the ethical issues. For example, Jordan, a manager at Acorn, described the discomfort and helplessness she felt when, as a student, she had witnessed behaviour that she considered 'horrendous', but which was 'brushed under the carpet' by her tutor when Jordan told her about it. She escalated a later protest to Ofsted, with more tangible results, but she resolved her own distress by leaving the nursery. As a student, she was powerless to challenge and resolve the unethical behaviour when her tutor was reluctant to believe her or to take action. In other cases, ethically correct behaviour was less obvious. Lyn, a manager at a nursery in a socially deprived area, described a practitioner being told by a parent from the travelling community that her husband had been arrested for armed robbery but that 'he didn't do it, it was his brother, but we're going to keep that between us'. Lyn and the practitioner 'sort of argued' about what they should do, and she described how they were 'just thinking about this child, you know, forget everything else'. They escalated their discussion to consult the nursery owner, Kate, and then they recalled the local authority safeguarding training that they had attended not long before: 'we were told … there's a police thing you can ring … even if you hear something that's hearsay'. On calling, anonymously, they were reassured by the response as the police 'were really grateful' for the information.

The dilemma in that situation was that Lyn and the practitioner were clearly very concerned about taking any action that would jeopardise the 'particularly good relationship' that had been built up with the mother who had confided in the practitioner, but they were also clear that they couldn't ethically ignore the information, even if it was technically hearsay. The sensemaking that took place was collective in that it involved the practitioner, the manager and the owner of the nursery, and although they had begun with different objectives, from protecting the parent to, in Lyn's words, 'doing the right thing' legally, they had all focused on what mattered for the child. Maintaining a good relationship with a difficult family was a very high priority, but helping to prevent a wrongful conviction and also alerting the police to the possible correct identity of the offender were also moral issues that needed to be resolved.

The sensemaking-intuition model (SIM) proposed by Sonenshein (2007) provides a useful three-stage framework of (1) issue construction, (2) intuitive judgement and (3) explanation and justification, which can be applied to the ethical sensemaking in the scenario described. The sensemaking began at the point when Lyn challenged the practitioner, saying 'I don't think I should tell you what she told me' – that is, when the individual moral concern was shared and explored. The dilemma was, first, whether to tell the police and, second, whether this could or should be done anonymously. Reflecting the first stage of the SIM, Lyn and the practitioner had constructed the issue together and articulated the desire to do the right thing, and Lyn and Kate acted as 'social actors' in helping the practitioner to test her interpretation of the situation, expanding her horizon from the relationship with the parent to the wider issue of criminal justice. The second stage of the SIM is the point at which individuals reach plausible interpretations and have an intuitive reaction which serves as a moral judgement, and that is the point where the SIM usefully recognises that 'affect can emerge prior to cognitions', with rationalising comprising the final stage of sensemaking Sonenshein (2007, p 1032). For Lyn and Kate, the immediate instinct was to refer the incident, while the practitioner's initial reaction was to protect her relationship with the family.

The social pressure from Lyn and Kate was clearly a factor in the practitioner's consenting to inform the police, and the third stage of the SIM, explaining and justifying the action taken, is demonstrated in Lyn's account after the event. She described it as 'putting all the pieces together ... we're pieces of a puzzle and where we can try and fit them we will ... but that's really difficult. You know, these people are not always nice people.' That final comment highlights another factor in the ethical sensemaking that wasn't articulated but was implicit in the description in that it was very evident that an anonymous tip-off was felt to be safer for the individuals making the call.

In this instance of ethical sensemaking, relationships were an important factor, highlighting the need to consider the implicit social processes that underpin individuals' responses to ethical issues. The relationship with the parent would have been jeopardised by an open breach of confidentiality, which could potentially have resulted in the child's removal from nursery, which was a safe place for him. The disclosure would not have been made at all if the practitioner had not already built that trusting relationship. The trusting relationships between the practitioner, her manager and the nursery owner were also apparent in the description of the debate about the right course of action and helped to achieve a consensus. At the heart of the process, there was also an explicit desire to 'do the right thing'.

The role of practitioner autonomy in tackling ethical slippage

Ethical slippage has been described as 'moments departing from expectations but not leading to clear breaches of ethical conduct' (Cutting and Peacock,

2021, abstract), and in early years practice, this might be seen in situations where a practitioner's tone of voice or physical handling of a child is not as sensitive and caring as the setting would expect but falls short of requiring disciplinary action or referral as a safeguarding concern. If unchallenged, however – which is more likely to be the case if the practitioner holds a senior role within the nursery – such uncaring, unethical practice may gradually be accepted as a norm to be tolerated. This is particularly dangerous when there are impressionable trainees, who may then themselves fail to develop a caring, empathetic attitude in their own practice. There may be a gap between ethical policies and ethics in practice, which rely on practitioner interpretations.

An individual practitioner may also find themselves in a dilemma if they disagree with a parent's instructions about how long their child should be allowed to sleep. Emily, for example, described her dilemma of whether to wake a child up after ten minutes in line with the parent's stipulation: 'Do we do the best for the child or do we do the best for the parent?' She recalled her compromise of letting the child sleep a little longer and then explaining to the parent that the child 'wouldn't wake up' until he'd been allowed to sleep a little longer. There was no doubt in Emily's mind about the correct course of action for the child: 'you and I both know that children need to be able to sleep for their brain to develop'. She added that she would try to give her 'professional opinion' to the parent about why she felt the child needed to be allowed to sleep. Similar dilemmas, involving balancing parental requests with children's needs, were voiced by other interviewees. These included the time when a father expressed concern about the role of a male practitioner (as described by Cara; see Chapter 4) and times where parents, usually fathers, complained about boys being allowed to dress up as ballerinas or Elsa from *Frozen*. In such cases, the practitioners' confidence about the need to challenge such gender stereotypes reflected the strength of a nursery community of practice. In cases of ethical sensemaking, the consensus between colleagues about what was 'right for the child' enabled practitioners to have confidence in their professional knowledge and to assert their professional identity .

At an organisational level, ethical slippage can arise when the requirement for efficient deployment of staff may conflict with the need to provide continuity of care for children. One example was described by Maya, an area manager, who had to deal with the aftermath when a nursery was acquired. Both staff and parents were upset that several staff were being redeployed to another nursery in the group, with no time to arrange transitions and with little regard to continuity of care for the children. Maya was left by the senior management to host a meeting for the aggrieved parents, and she described the experience of having to lie to them about the quality of nursery practice: 'I'm sitting in a parent meeting telling them how great the nursery was. And I'm thinking, my conscience isn't clear. I can't do this …

So I called it a day.' The last straw for her was having to support nursery managers who were unable to meet mandatory staffing ratios but who had been told 'to manage it' and not use agency staff. Similarly, the requirement for inclusive practice in the admission of children with additional needs often causes resourcing difficulties for early years settings when time and staffing resources are taken up in order to accommodate the children safely.

Autonomy and agency are important factors in ethical decision-making, and there is some evidence that people are more susceptible to accept unethical behaviour if they have lower levels of confidence, independence and autonomy (see Trevino, 1986). Confidence is needed to challenge poor practice or unethical policies, and if people have higher levels of independence and autonomy, they are more reliant on their personal moral or ethical codes. Performance measures, which reflect organisational purpose and mission, can affect practitioners' and managers' confidence in their own beliefs about what is right. Also, individual behaviour is embedded in networks of interpersonal relationships (Granovetter, 1985), and practitioners are influenced by colleagues, whether because of roles and power relationships or because the individual is respected and admired.

Professional identity is a key factor in determining levels of confidence and autonomy. There has been some debate about whether autonomy is compatible with relationality (Mackenzie and Stoljar, 2000), but this is an issue of degree rather than an either-or, and there is a recognition by care ethicists that 'autonomy and independence are about the capacity for self-determination rather than the expectation of individual self-sufficiency' (Williams, 2001, p 487). The kind of autonomy that may enable practitioners to tackle ethical slippage is perhaps best explained with an example. Dealing with the shortfall in funding for the 'free' childcare entitlement has thrown up ethical conundrums for many, especially when the government responded to protests by saying that additional charges could be made for activities, meals and consumables but those charges should be voluntary. In my research interviews, several practitioners described how they disregarded official guidance in order to ensure that all children received equal provision. The situation worsened, as the 'optional extras' requirement has been included in provider agreements with local authorities, with the expectation that a menu of additional costs to the basic funded care hours is provided to families.

In this situation, a case of ethical slippage on a national scale, many nurseries are being forced to charge for activities for forest school sessions, for example. The ethical issue here is that a two-tier provision is created whereby only children whose parents can afford the additional charge would be able to attend. Many settings are challenging the guidance that suggests families should be allowed to provide their own packed lunches or consumables, rather than pay a charge for these to be provided. This is not just due to the logistical nightmare of additional administration, and the health and safety implications of packed lunches, but having two separate types of meals being provided would be to impose a lack of inclusion on settings. This has caused a great deal of anguish, especially for those operating in low-income areas, as there is a recognition that many families would understandably opt for the lowest cost option. One of the problems with packed lunches, as mentioned in Chapter 1, is that there is a cultural capital associated with mealtime rituals, which would be missed with packed lunches where there is no sharing of dishes, use of cutlery or exposure to a wide variety of dishes from different cultures. Practitioner autonomy in this situation is likely to be limited, but a collective voice of protest might yet force the policy makers to pay attention to the unintended consequences of their well-intentioned but unwittingly uncaring actions. Free school meals are universal in UK primary schools, so it's also inconsistent not to include these for preschool children.

The impact of ethical sensemaking and sensegiving

Sensemaking and sensegiving can be valuable tools for ethical leaders, and ethical sensemaking can also be a form of organisational learning. Ethical sensemaking can help to balance the potential conflict between organisational drivers for success and practitioners' concern for excellence; both are important, but they need to be balanced. One way nursery managers can engage in sensemaking to embed ethical practices is through 'social poetics', described as 'relationally responsive dialogue' in which 'meaning may be created between people, both in the moment of speech and after the moment in reflection upon it' (Shotter and Cunliffe, 2003, p 28). Learning as reflective/reflexive dialogue involves 'reworking learning from a cognitive to a dialogical process' (Cunliffe, 2002, p 36). Here, managers and practitioners may be instinctively struck by a situation in an embodied, tacit way and then make sense of, rationalise and agree responses through dialogue with colleagues and through further reflection. When situations involve feelings, which is often the case when working with babies and young children, 'work discussion' can provide a valuable tool to recognise the emotional work involved and support the well-being of early years practitioners (Elfer, 2024).

Sensemaking may not just be about whether behaviour or actions are ethical – in the early years sector a practitioner's concerns about a range of issues may trigger a sensemaking process in which they consider whether their concern needs to be addressed at an organisational level or within the immediate team. The ensuing dialogue or professional discourse is an example of what Cunliffe describes as a change in focus 'from a purely theoretical *talking about practice* as an uninvolved observer (outside-in), to include a dialogical, responsive *talking in practice* (inside-out)' (2002, p 46, emphasis in original). Dialogical opportunities were described by the interviewees in my research.

For example, Acorn manager Kim described learning from a previous line manager who demonstrated and then discussed how to involve children in everyday tasks such as finding boots or tissues. That sensegiving by her colleague enabled Kim to extend her understanding of appropriate activities for children. It allowed her to change her perception of the task of finding missing objects as being separate from her role as an educator so that, instead, she saw it as an activity she could involve children in to jointly problem-solve. Kim's lively account of the experience also provided an insight into her new-found talent for turning mundane tasks into examples of sustained shared thinking (Siraj-Blatchford, 2009; Howard et al, 2018).

Within a nursery situation, and in the context of sensemaking as absorbed coping, described earlier (see Sandberg and Tsoukas, 2020), several interviewees commented on the need to explain the rationale behind practices to new and inexperienced practitioners. In one example, deputy manager Amy was 'blown away' by her induction into the respectful care approach, saying that she used to 'go behind a child and just wipe their nose' and hadn't ever considered the need for more sensitivity when undertaking these sorts of care practices, which, she reflected, 'just seems so obvious'. Nose-wiping techniques offer a micro-level example of how an ethic of care may or may not be embedded in nursery practices, demonstrating the need for practitioners to understand the impact of physical actions in a more reflective way in order to implement a change of habit. The arrow in the model of ethical sensegiving in Figure 7.1 indicates the impact of sensegiving, illustrated by the nursery manager transforming Amy's practice to be more consistently sensitive.

The practice of sensegiving is also illustrated in Vignette 7.1. My perception in this case was that there were high levels of leader sensegiving within the nursery, which led to a successfully embedded culture of high-quality childcare and early education. In other interviews, practitioners described their personal commitment to ethical practice in settings that were not always supportive of it. Low levels of ethical sensegiving, in some nurseries, led to poor practice where practitioners also had low ethical awareness, while fragmentary pockets of ethical practice were evident where individual practitioners attempted to maintain their own ethical standards. Sensegiving as a process could be identified in the descriptions of managers and senior practitioners who were training or supervising others, but was not something that was described by practitioners who were not in positions of power or influence. Their individual sensemaking of the nursery culture and practices led to an acceptance and tolerance of poor practice, a narrowing of focus to ensuring that their personal practice was ethical or, in several cases, a move to a different nursery that they perceived to have higher standards.

Sensegiving clearly resonates with the values articulation work discussed earlier. A common way of training practitioners in early years settings is by role-modelling the desired behaviours and skills, but a more discursive approach is required for communicating an understanding of *why* a practice should be done in a certain way. The risk otherwise is that a nappy changing routine, done sensitively and ethically, might be interpreted by an observer as unnecessarily time-consuming if it is not accompanied by sensegiving or values articulation to explain the importance of a relational, attentive approach, thus falling into 'fragmented ethical sensemaking', shown in the lower right quadrant of Figure 7.1 (Maitlis, 2005, p 32).

Ethical sensemaking can provide a tool to support ethical decision-making, and in terms of the ethic of care, this relates to Noddings' (2002; 2013) assertion that 'ethical caring' requires a more deliberate intent to the 'natural caring' of relatives and those close to us. Tronto similarly observes that the biggest challenge for care is that 'we care most for the people who are closest to us, observing that 'we think of care as natural, it isn't. We have to learn how to do it, and how to do it better. And part of doing it better is being trained to see things differently' (in Parra Jounou and Tronto, 2024, p 276).

In some cases, empathy can counteract ethical practices. In the inspirational *Humankind*, Rutger Bregman (2020) examines the way in which camaraderie and friendship can override ideological arguments, leading to Nazi troops having extremely low desertion rates in the Second World War despite millions of propaganda leaflets being dropped to explain how their position was hopeless and their ideology despicable. His account of the 'Baby Lab' experiments explained that they initially gave the impression that infants naturally preferred 'helper' puppets over badly behaved puppets but that later experiments also showed that toddlers are very sensitive to differences in others and are naturally tribal, preferring other children that are similar to themselves – so in Bregman's words, infants and toddlers are 'basically friendly, but with xenophobic tendencies' (2020, p 216). This depressing conclusion is at odds with the otherwise positive message in his book, but it does alert us to the need to proactively engage children in activities that enhance their understanding of other ethnicities and cultures. Children learn from their peers and the adults around them. A child's reaction to spiders is likely to be influenced by whether adults around them react with fear or curiosity when one appears, and children need to be supported to react with empathy and respect when encountering difference of any kind. Children who have played with children with disabilities at nursery, for example, tend to be more confident and empathetic when encountering other people with mobility or sensory impairments.

Embodied ethical sensemaking

By combining ethical sensemaking and embodied practice, I have developed the concept of embodied ethical sensemaking (shown in Figure 7.2), which

Figure 7.2: Embodied ethical sensemaking in early years practice

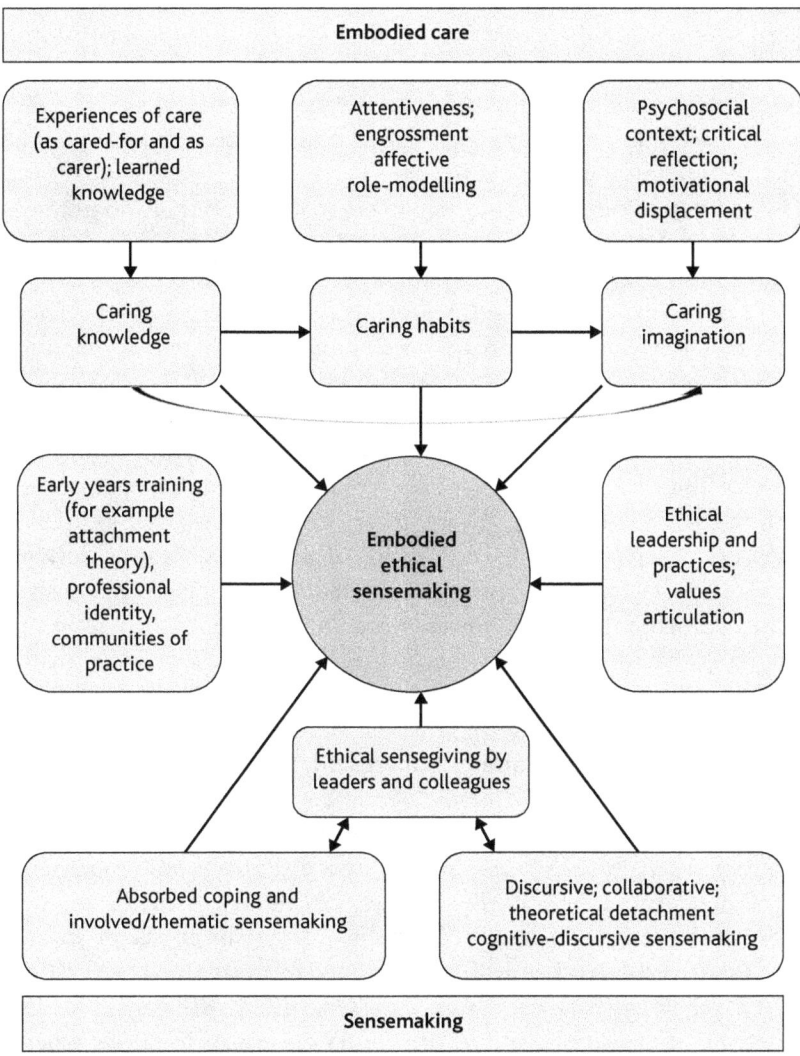

I believe provides an insight into one way that an ethic of care can be implemented in early years provision. In coming up with this concept, I used the sensemaking models outlined in Figure 7.1 and Table 7.1, and I applied Hamington's concept of embodied care and its three components, discussed in Chapter 5. I also drew on examples from my research data.

I begin with a predisposition for ethical care, as exemplified in the interview data, with practitioners consistently talking about a 'right' way to do things and the need to put children's needs first. The first component of embodied care, *caring knowledge*, often stems from an ethical predisposition and is likely to be influenced by early experiences of being cared for and later experiences of caring for others, both within childcare and in lived experiences outside the workplace. Training and professional development contributes to this knowledge, particularly in terms of understanding child development, attachment theory and awareness of the impact of stress and distress. Caring knowledge is then habituated in care activities, and caring habits are a form of caring knowledge.

Caring habits in early years practice mean that practitioners do not need to stop to think about their bodily positioning, tone of voice and attentiveness to the children in their care, as these have become embodied. Caring habits necessarily include the attentiveness of Noddings' (2010a) concept of engrossment, and the empathic intersubjectivity between practitioners and children becomes instinctive. At this point, there is a correlation with the absorbed coping (see Sandberg and Tsoukas, 2020) of sensemaking that takes place continually in nurseries in the responses made to changes in children's emotional well-being and in the skilful implementation of care practices and daily routines. Although primarily determined by individual agency, caring habits and the sensemaking of absorbed coping are influenced by organisational features, which may determine staffing levels, consistency in staff deployment and whether leaders and colleagues engage in ethical sensegiving. Embodied caring habits also allow practitioners and managers to challenge instances of unethical practice (such as when Tara responded to the upset baby in a highchair in Chapter 3), which illustrates the involved-deliberate type of sensemaking (Sandberg and Tsoukas, 2020; see Table 7.1).

Habitual behaviours can easily become care-less, which is why the emphasis on *caring habits* is important for ethical care practices. As observed by Dewey, we acquire the morality of our social group, and 'the essence of habit is an acquired predisposition to ways or modes of response ... Habit means special sensitiveness or accessibility to certain classes of stimuli ... rather than bare recurrence of specific acts. It means will.' (2020, p 16). When a child's cry is heard within a nursery, those with caring habits will instinctively move to respond to the child's distress or to check whether a colleague is already doing so. If uncaring habits are formed collectively, a culture of insensitivity is created.

Caring imagination is the aspect of embodied care that moves beyond direct primary experience. It relies heavily on empathy and motivational displacement. Critical reflection is an essential ingredient in caring imagination, according to Hamington (2004), and this is also a factor in detached-deliberate sensemaking. The psychosocial context is important here too, with the influence of colleagues and social pressures inevitably affecting the sensemaking process. Sandberg and Tsoukas (2020) describe such sensemaking as primarily cognitive-discursive, but the dilemma described earlier of the parent potentially being involved in an armed robbery did not involve a simple moral decision. The practitioner had 'a particularly good relationship' with the mother, who was part of a traveller community that 'don't tell outside people what goes on within their group', so the risk of jeopardising that trust between parent and practitioner, and the potential impact on the child's care, had an emotional element that went beyond moral rationalising. Similarly, the debates that took place in the sector about drop-offs and collections post COVID-19 showed that the theoretical detachment type of sensemaking (see Table 7.1) is not purely analytical, as the participants displayed heightened emotions when expressing their views. Some felt that separations and reunions of parents and children at the door, enforced by COVID-19 social distancing rules, should be continued. Others vehemently disagreed. Recognising the embodiment of ethical intentions in an individual's caring knowledge, caring habits and caring imagination is helpful in understanding the difference between childcare practices that could be described as non-caring or acaring (see Hamington, 2004) and care practices that are warm, sensitive and thoughtful.

8

Making childcare sustainable: a care manifesto

The need for a (child)care manifesto

In this final chapter, I summarise the argument outlined in this book and explain what I think needs to be done to embed an ethic of care in early years care and education, which, I conclude, would support all three pillars of sustainability: financial, environmental and social. Many countries are facing economic difficulties, increasingly critical impacts of the climate crisis, rising inequality and a breakdown in social cohesion, but in raising the next generation to be more caring, we can each of us make a difference. The early years sector has been undervalued for many years, but with a moral and political will to care, better support for caregivers and more understanding of what high-quality care should be, the impact of an embedded ethic of care could improve the lives of children, their families and the early years workforce, as well as having a ripple effect on wider society.

In the first chapter, I explained how and why the problems of schoolification, marketisation and the undervaluing of childcare arose and why we need to be more aware of the terminology being used. I explored the problem of marketisation further in Chapter 2, arguing that the commodification of childcare is a greater concern than the funding issue. I showed that learning and development opportunities for the early years workforce are a critical feature of high-quality childcare, and I compared the approach of different countries to suggest where the UK might learn from best (and worst) practice. In Chapter 3, I explored the organisational level, arguing that social purpose is more effective than profitability in driving higher quality and in creating caring a workplace culture. I took the analysis of care ethics to the individual level in Chapter 4, explaining that care ethics originated in maternalism and describing how a relational approach and the adoption of care as an organising principle can embed high quality in early years settings.

In the second half of the book, I took a deep dive into embodied care practices, arguing in Chapter 5 for a greater appreciation and understanding of the importance of touch, tacit knowledge, the role of emotions and the role of pace. In Chapter 6, I explored aspects of sociomateriality which have an impact in nurseries, from furniture to personal protective equipment and play equipment. I also emphasised the importance of the outdoor environment and the critical role of the adult. Finally, in Chapter 7, I presented a model of embodied ethical sensemaking. I explained that sensegiving can be a valuable leadership practice in articulating and embedding ethical values, and I highlighted that practitioner autonomy is important for preventing ethical slippage.

In this final chapter, I explain how each of these arguments fits into the vision of a more sustainable future, placing care front and centre in each of the three pillars of sustainability. Embedding an ethic of care in early years settings is, I believe, the best way to support high-quality and inclusive practice, but this needs to be supported by policy makers, organisation leaders and managers, and those working directly with our very precious children, the next generation.

Care ethics and the pillars of sustainability

Sustainability is at the heart of an ethic of care, particularly as it applies to social and financial sustainability as well as ecology and the climate crisis. Ethical caring means caring beyond one's personal sphere, which means that caring for other people, in all parts of society, and caring for the environment should be a natural extension of our care for ourselves, our friends and family, and the children and colleagues in our workplace. Our natural world requires protection, and if we care about children, who are the next generation, we must also care about the world they are inheriting. Sustainability is often conceptualised as either a three-pillar model or three circles, concentric or intersecting, and although the genesis of sustainable development goes back several decades, the modern concept was not formed until the late 20th century (Purvis et al, 2019). The content of the three pillars or circles is consistently shown as economic, social and environmental, as shown in Figure 8.1, and these match the evolution of the 'triple bottom line' (Elkington, 1997), which is also sometimes referred to as people, planet and profits.

The application of care ethics to these concepts focuses attention on priorities and responsibility, and all three aspects of sustainability are inherently political. The ethics of care is also political, highlighting power relations and inequality, and childcare is often unpaid and linked to women's inequalities (Williams, 2018). Transnational crises of care and migration affect the early years sector as well as wider society, and the limited human and physical resources of the planet are the wider context to more local struggles with funding, the workforce and the pressure on families to work and rear their children.

Joan Tronto argues that '[t]he great challenge of democratic life is to provide for economic production – which produces inequality – and at the same time to recognise everyone as equal participants in their society' (2013, p xi). If we add the need to care for and respect the planet too, we have the three pillars of sustainability, and as the ethic of care is also relational in nature, it recognises the interdependence that is so crucial for sustainable practices

Figure 8.1: The three circles of sustainability

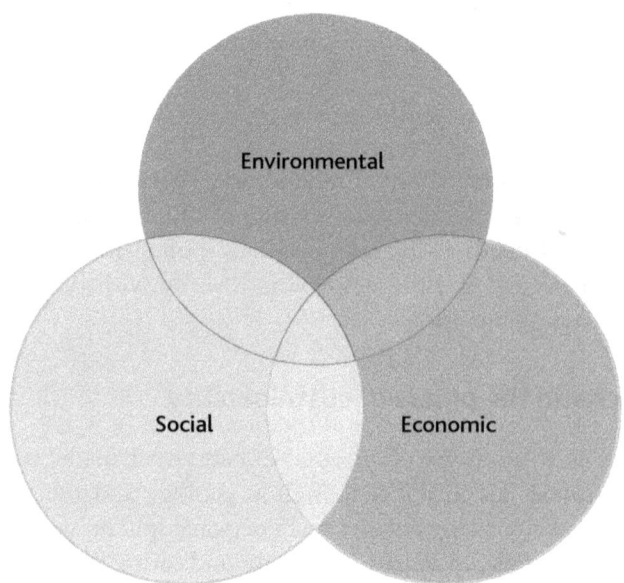

to be effective. In terms of early years provision, it also becomes clear that organisations which are purpose driven may find it easier to ensure that the profit driver does not overshadow social and environmental sustainability. Tronto asserts that a preoccupation with economic production and growth has left care as a secondary consideration, and that *caring with* needs to be a responsibility that citizens take seriously. Caring for others and for the planet is in fact an easy ask within the early years sector, and I hope to show how an ethic of care enables sustainable practices to become embedded.

Financial sustainability in a two-tier sector

Financial sustainability is a topical issue for childcare providers, not just in the UK but also in other countries. The Australian company ABC Learning became the world's largest for-profit childcare provider after a period of rapid growth and flotation on what was then the Australian Stock Exchange in 2001. The group was commercially driven, targeting high-income communities, and it dominated the childcare market in Australia, which had adopted demand-side funding in 2000, after abandoning subsidies for not-for-profit provision. ABC Learning collapsed into insolvency in 2008, at which point it had approximately 16,000 employees, who were caring for over 100,000 children. The government had to spend millions of dollars to bail the company out, as it was by that point providing 30 per cent of the country's childcare places (Penn, 2013; Sumsion, 2013).

In the UK, a research study by Simon et al (2022) found that private-for-profit childcare companies were characterised by acquisitions, mergers and indebtedness, and that they tended to be dominated by highly leveraged financial models, similar to those used by ABC Learning. The report identified a 'heavy reliance on private equity to underwrite company expansion and a contradictory narrative of "growth through loss-making"', in some cases making profits at the level of the holding company while making losses at the subsidiary level (Simon et al, 2022, p 44). From an ethical perspective, the report also contains an example of carewashing in the reporting of a charitable foundation established by one of the largest companies, with the foundation paying more to the company to cover staff time in support of the foundation than the company itself donated to the charity (Simon et al, 2022, p 47). In both the ABC Learning example and in the UK research study, staffing costs in private-for-profit childcare companies were criticised for being lower than sector averages.

The crisis in financial sustainability for nurseries in the early years sector in the UK is not a universal one. There are many very profitable nurseries, and they have one thing in common – they are situated in affluent areas and charge high fees to families. The nurseries that are struggling, or even closing due to not being financially sustainable, are almost all unable to charge high fees or are too small to benefit from any economies of scale. My argument is that an ethic of care, and the use of ethical sensemaking, would help to address the systemic inequalities in the sector. At the level of government policy, the consequences of funding policies would be thought-through, taking account of feedback from providers and families. Organisations would hopefully be incentivised to invest in their staff teams and in their professional development, and financial support would enable provision to be sustainable in areas of economic disadvantage.

One of the recommendations coming out of Simon et al's (2022) research into private-for-profit childcare provision was that the government should explore social enterprise and charity-run nursery models, partly because they are committed to reinvesting their surpluses back into their organisations. The report also noted the stable financial structure of the hybrid model operated by one large provider that is employee owned. However, as noted, all the for-profit organisations were observed to target high-income locations for their provision, suggesting that social sustainability and inclusion is restricted to the third sector, as I explore next.

Social sustainability and inclusion in the early years sector

The concept of social sustainability focuses on how to meet the needs of individuals and societies within a sustainable framework, recognising the need for social justice. The 'Doughnut Economics' model (Raworth, 2017) illustrates the need for a 'social foundation' as well as an 'ecological ceiling' and stresses the need for social equity in having access to education, income and work, networks, a political voice, peace and justice. Raworth calls the sweet spot inside the two boundaries 'the safe and just space for humanity' and suggests social sustainability is about ensuring this can be created and sustained. Sustainability can be seen as a foundational practice that overlaps both economic and social justice (Whipps, 2012), and it is helpful to use an ethics of care approach to recognise the centrality of care and interdependence in efforts to embed sustainability in organisations (Williams, 2018). Raising the social value of care, including care of babies and young children, helps to raise the political and economic value of care and to recognise the way in which care sustains and supports healthy societies. In the world of early years, the importance of caring for the youngest members of society is not just applicable to childcare within nurseries and other early years settings, but about how families and early years professionals are supported to care effectively and to achieve a sustainable work–life balance. Care is a social practice, and the sharing of caring responsibilities between early years settings and families is a core component of ethical early years practice.

The way in which social sustainability is supported in early years can most clearly be seen in inclusive practice. The principle of inclusion underpins all good early years provision, and early years settings being able to support families who have children requiring additional help to access provision is one way of avoiding the consequences of children with special educational needs and disabilities (SEND) not being able to access early intervention. Families with children with SEND are often disadvantaged in terms of being able to continue their normal working lives, as funding from local authorities is usually limited to school hours and term-time attendance. When children with SEND are enabled to enjoy equal access to high-quality provision, there are also benefits for the other children within the setting, as they gain an understanding of how the lives of other children may differ from their own. Similarly, children from diverse backgrounds and cultures, and with differing home languages, can enrich the social environment of the setting and help to develop the understanding of all children about the lives of others and to embed mutually respectful and caring behaviours.

For all children, early years settings can help to support the links between different agencies and between education and health professionals. Several of my interviewees noted that early years professionals are often perceived by parents as friendlier and more approachable than staff in other agencies, and in nurseries in areas of economic deprivation, there were many accounts of additional support being given to help address families experiencing poverty and difficult home situations. For example, Hannah, head of early years in a charitable social enterprise, asserted her belief that 'if you can make a difference in a very small way, it goes a long way'. She added: 'I'm emotional because it really affects me, because, you know, our job in early years is to have a voice for these young families.' Many of my interviewees expressed frustration at the lack of recognition from the government about the way in which early years settings support the wider family, and thereby improve social sustainability. In contrast, I also heard accounts of nurseries where managers were strongly discouraged from taking on children with additional needs, or 'funded-only' children, as they were perceived to incur additional costs and staff time, which might have an impact on levels of profitability.

Embracing an ethic of care can empower early years practitioners to challenge uncaring practices, and Hamington's (2004; 2015) three dimensions of embodied care, described in Chapter 5, offer a way of extending circles of care: 'caring imagination' addresses the need to extend empathy and understanding to those with whom we are less familiar, which describes the essence of inclusive practice; 'caring knowledge' captures the way in which information about others can be acquired implicitly through our interactions with them; and 'caring habits' includes the subtle but important awareness of body language, tone of voice and attentive listening. All three can help to highlight an awareness of unintentional microaggressions, which are an example of uncaring habits, and they can provide a ' path through which responsiveness to the human aspects of sustainable practice might occur' (Simola, 2012, p 474).

Environmental sustainability and the role of care in the climate crisis

The feminist theory of care described by Fisher and Tronto suggests that caring should be viewed as 'a species activity that includes everything that we do to maintain, continue, and repair our "world" so that we can live in it as well as possible. That world includes our bodies, our selves, and our environment, all of which we seek to interweave in a complex, life-sustaining web' (1990, p 40). Caring for the environment has become an increasingly urgent need in the face of the climate crisis, and an ethic of care provides a framework through which to approach it. Fisher and Tronto identify four 'ability factors', which they describe as specific preconditions of caring activity, and these are appropriate both for childcare practices and education for sustainability.

The first of these is time, which I discussed in Chapter 5 in relation to unhurried care and slow pedagogy, but is also critical for sustainability. For instance, fast food is associated with both unhealthy eating and single-use items, while the slow food movement is a global, grass-roots movement that began in Italy in 1989 and promotes sustainable and healthy food for all (see Slow Food in the UK, nd). The use of cars for short journeys is also an issue of pace being prioritised over both the environment and the health benefits of walking or cycling to work or nursery.

The second ability factor, material resources, as I discussed in Chapter 6, is essential in creating caring environments. And the use of sustainably sourced and long-lasting materials make an important contribution to a nursery's sustainability.

Knowledge and skill were identified as the third and fourth ability factors, and these are as important for embedding sustainability as they are for childcare practices. Knowledge of how best to make a difference (and why) is a key requirement for successful implementation, as is skill, particularly in persuading colleagues to embrace eco-friendly practices and in identifying appropriate activities to engage children's interest and promote their understanding of how to care for the environment and why they should do so.

Tronto's (1993) four phases of care, introduced in Chapter 3 and discussed further in Chapter 4, can also be applied to sustainability. 'Caring about' the environment is an essential starting point, and 'taking care of' describes how early years professionals might take responsibility within their setting to implement sustainable practices. 'Caregiving' for the environment and for living creatures and plants by children and early years professionals is the most practical and effective way to engage children's interest and to enhance their understanding of the natural world, and 'care receiving' can be seen in the feedback loop from that caregiving – wilting plants that haven't been watered provide a graphic illustration of the impact of withdrawing care, just as those that flourish and grow when nurtured by children and their carers illustrate the impact of providing care. Embedding sustainable habits within a nursery can have a wide-ranging impact on children and their families, and a heightened awareness of environmental impacts of everyday practices is a natural extension of caring attentiveness. Tronto's (2013) later addition of a fifth phase of 'caring with' also speaks to the need for sustainability to be a collective endeavour.

The importance of experiential knowledge in shaping our attitude to sustainability was articulated eloquently by Richard Louv: 'We cannot protect something we do not love, we cannot love what we do not know, and we cannot know what we do not see. Or hear. Or sense' (2005, p 104). A critical factor in cultivating a love of nature and a desire and intention to care for it is giving children first-hand experience. The importance of children having sensory access to the natural world is recognised by Montessori in an often-quoted passage attributed to her:

> Let the children be free; encourage them; let them run outside when it is raining; let them remove their shoes when they find a puddle of water; and, when the grass of the meadows is damp with dew, let them run on it and trample it with their bare feet; let them rest peacefully when a tree invites them to sleep beneath its shade.

The (child)care manifesto for the early years

So what do we need to do? First, at the level of government policy, we need politicians to *care about* children, families and the workforce by formulating policies that do not jeopardise inclusive practice (yes, I mean the iniquity of 'optional extras'). We need them to *take care of* the workforce by ensuring that funding incentivises providers to provide professional development opportunities and career progression, as well as ensuring that funding levels recognise the need for professional pay scales. We need policy makers who genuinely listen to the sector and learn from best practices, both in the UK and in other countries, and who ensure that curriculum guidance is not simply focused on measurable educational outcomes, but recognises that high-quality early care and education is a preparation for life, not just schooling. Also, to achieve equal parenting and a gender-balanced workforce, politicians need to recognise the need for more generous shared parental leave.

At the organisational level, leaders and managers need to *care about* their workforce and for the children in their nurseries more than they care about their profitability. *Taking care of* their workforce means taking responsibility for ensuring that early years professionals are treated like professionals, with training opportunities during the working day and the time and resources needed to care effectively for the children and to support their families. Organisational policies need to be developed to prioritise children's needs over operational efficiency, and budgets need to focus on what is needed to deliver high-quality provision, not just what will 'sell' the nursery in a competitive market. Leaders can use sensemaking and sensegiving to heighten an awareness of organisational purpose and to ensure that inclusive practice is deeply embedded, with *all* children receiving the same high quality of care and early years education.

Practitioners already have a good understanding of how to prioritise children's care needs, but having more self-awareness of their professional status may enable them to challenge policies and poor practice. Ethical sensemaking may help them to understand the importance of reflective practice and *care receiving*, and it may also increase their awareness of tacit knowledge, embodied care and the impact that apparently simple care routines can have on children. An embedded ethic of care relies on teamwork and the need to care about and for colleagues. It also supports practitioners to extend their care ethic to the wider environment and to educate children about how to care for themselves, other people and the natural world.

Parents and carers have a role to play too. A genuine partnership between early years practitioners and children's families provides a bedrock of care for children that optimises their chances of experiencing consistent, loving, respectful care. Children need good role models so that they can grow into caring, responsible citizens and experience the rewards of showing care to others – other children, nursery staff, family members, pets, plants and the wider natural environment. A caring disposition is something to celebrate and be proud of, and it will be a long-term source of emotional stability and self-esteem. To care is to be human, and attentive, relational, embodied care can never be provided by artificial intelligence or by robots. The ability to care is an essential basis for successful relationships and for a caring and connected society.

My care manifesto, then, can be summed up in ten points, and the reversal of that infamous slogan on Melania Trump's jacket. 'I really do care. Do you?'

1. Care is a moral and political value, and an ethic of care provides a blueprint for ethical practice in early years provision.
2. Early childhood care and education is a preparation for life, not for school.
3. Children are not a commodity, and their needs should be prioritised over profit.
4. Purpose-driven organisations facilitate high-quality and inclusive practice.
5. Early-years professionals need to be properly valued and supported.
6. More awareness and understanding is needed on the importance of tacit knowledge, the influence of pace, the role of sociomateriality and the nature of embodied care.
7. Sensemaking and sensegiving are valuable tools for ethical leadership.
8. The implementation of an ethic of care embeds inclusive practice.
9. An ethic of care encourages economic, social and environmental sustainability.
10. Care *is* education, if done well. Children need to experience care and to have caring role models to become caring themselves, and their ability to care – for themselves, for others and for the natural world – is critical for the future well-being of us all.

References

Ahmed, S. (2004) *The Cultural Politics of Emotion*, Edinburgh University Press.

Ailwood, J. (2007) 'Mothers, teachers, maternalism and early childhood education and care: some historical connections', *Contemporary Issues in Early Childhood*, 8(2): 157–65. doi: 10.2304/ciec.2007.8.2.157

Allen, G. (2011) *Early Intervention: Smart Investment, Massive Savings. The Second Independent Report to Her Majesty's Government*, HM Government.

All-Party Parliamentary Group on a Fit and Healthy Childhood (2020) *Wellbeing and Nurture: Physical and Emotional Security in Childhood*, All-Party Parliamentary Group on a Fit and Healthy Childhood.

Anastasiadis, S. and Zeyen, A. (2022) 'Families under pressure: the costs of vocational calling, and what can be done about them', *Work, Employment and Society*, 36(5): 841–57. doi: 10.1177/0950017020980986

André, K. and Pache, A.C. (2016) 'From caring entrepreneur to caring enterprise: addressing the ethical challenges of scaling up social enterprises', *Journal of Business Ethics*, 133(4): 659–75. doi: 10.1007/s10551-014-2445-8

Archer, N. (2021) '"I have this subversive curriculum underneath": narratives of micro resistance in early childhood education', *Journal of Early Childhood Research*, advance online publication. doi: 10.1177/1476718X211059907

Archer, N. and Merrick, B. (2020) *Getting the Balance Right: Quality and Quantity in Early Education & Childcare*, The Sutton Trust. Available at: www.suttontrust.com/our-research/getting-the-balance-right

Argyris, C.A. and Schon, D.A. (1974) *Theory in Practice*, Jossey-Bass.

Baraister, L. (2009) *Maternal Encounters: The Ethics of Interruption*, Routledge.

Barnes, M. (2019) 'Contesting and transforming care: an introduction to a critical ethics of care', in R. Langford (ed) *Theorizing Feminist Ethics of Care in Early Childhood Practice: Possibilities and Danger*, Bloomsbury, pp 17–36.

Bell, D.C. and Richard, A.J. (2000) 'Caregiving: the forgotten element in attachment', *Psychological Inquiry*, 11(2): 69–83. doi: 10.1207/S15327965PLI1102_01

Bone, J. (2019) 'Ghosts of the material world in early childhood education: furniture matters', *Contemporary Issues in Early Childhood*, 20(2): 133–45. doi: 10.1177/1463949117749599

Bonetti, S. (2019) *The Early Years Workforce in England: A Comparative Analysis Using the Labour Force Survey*, Education Policy Institute. Available at: https://epi.org.uk/wp-content/uploads/2019/01/The-early-years-workforce-in-England_EPI.pdf

Bowden, P. (1997) *Caring: Gender-Sensitive Ethics*, Routledge.

Bowden, P. (2000) 'An "ethic of care" in clinical settings: encompassing "feminine" and "feminist" perspectives', *Nursing Philosophy*, 1(1): 36–49. doi: 10.1046/j.1466-769x.2000.00009.x

Bowlby, J. (1969) *Attachment*, Pimlico.

Bowlby, R. (2007) 'Babies and toddlers in non-parental daycare can avoid stress and anxiety if they develop a lasting secondary attachment bond with one carer who is consistently accessible to them', *Attachment and Human Development*, 9(4): 307–19. doi: 10.1080/14616730701711516

Boyer, K., Reimer, S. and Irvine, L. (2013) 'The nursery workspace, emotional labour and contested understandings of commoditised childcare in the contemporary UK', *Social and Cultural Geography*, 14(5): 517–40. doi: 10.1080/14649365.2012.710913

Bregman, R. (2020) *Humankind: A Hopeful History*, Bloomsbury.

Bruce, T. (2021) *Friedrich Froebel*, Bloomsbury.

Chai, Y., Nandi, A. and Heymann, J. (2018) 'Does extending the duration of legislated paid maternity leave improve breastfeeding practices? Evidence from 38 low-income and middle-income countries', *BMJ Global Health*, 3(5): art e001032. doi: 10.1136/bmjgh-2018-001032

Chatzidakis, A., Hakim, J., Littler, J., Rottenberg, C. and Segal, L. (2020), *The Care Manifesto: The Politics of Interdependence*, Verso.

Chodorow, N. (1978) *The Reproduction of Mothering: Psychoanalysis and the Sociology of Gender*, University of California Press.

Chodorow, N.J. (2000) 'Reflections on *The Reproduction of Mothering*—twenty years later', *Studies in Gender and Sexuality*, 1(4): 337–48. doi: 10.1080/15240650109349163

Clare, A. (2012) *Creating a Learning Environment for Babies and Toddlers*, SAGE.

Clark, A. (2023) *Slow Knowledge and the Unhurried Child*, Routledge.

Cloyes, K.G. (2002) 'Agonizing care: care ethics, agonistic feminism and a political theory of care', *Nursing Inquiry*, 9(3): 203–14. doi: 10.1046/j.1440-1800.2002.00147.x

Conkbayir, M. (2023) *The Neuroscience of the Developing Child*, Routledge.

Crowley, J., Wilson, C., Moller Vallgarda, L., Speight, S. and Bhatti, S. (2025) *Study of Early Education and Development (SEED): Impact Report on Early Education Use and Child Outcomes at Key Stage 2*, Department for Education.

Cunliffe, A.L. (2002) 'Reflexive dialogical practice in management learning', *Management Learning*, 33(1): 35–61. doi: 10.1177/135050760233

Cutting, K. and Peacock, S. (2021) 'Making sense of "slippages": re-evaluating ethics for digital research with children and young people', *Children's Geographies*, 1–13. doi: 10.1080/14733285.2021.1906404

Dachler, H.P. and Hosking, D.M. (1995) 'The primacy of relations in socially constructing organizational realities', in D.M. Hosking, H.P. Dachler and K.J. Gergler (eds) *Management and Organizations: Relationship Alternatives to Individualism*, Avebury, pp 1–28.

D'Adderio, L. (2021) 'Materiality and routine dynamics', in M.S. Feldman, B.T. Pentland, L. D'Adderio, K. Dittrich, C. Rerup and D. Seidel (eds) *Cambridge Handbook of Routine Dynamics*, Cambridge University Press, pp 85–101.

References

Department for Education (2025a) *Early Years Foundation Stage Statutory Framework: For Group and School-Based Providers*, Department for Education. Available at: www.gov.uk/government/publications/early-years-foundation-stage-framework--2

Department for Education (2025b) *The Experience-Based Route for Early Years*, Department for Education. Available at: https://assets.publishing.service.gov.uk/media/68b1c98211b4ded2da19fc80/Experience-based_route_for_early_years_non-statutory_guidance_Sept_25.pdf

Department for Education (2025c) *Giving Every Child the Best Start Start in Life*, CP 1362, Department for Education. Available at: https://assets.publishing.service.gov.uk/media/689b39d55555fb89cf3f5e7d/Giving_every_child_the_best_start_in_life_web_version.pdf

Dewey, J. (2020 [1922]) *Human Nature and Conduct*, Bibliotech Press.

Dreyfus, H.L. and Dreyfus, S.E. (1991) 'Towards a phenomenology of ethical expertise', *Human Studies*, 14(4): 229–50.

Dudek, M. (2013) *Nurseries: A Design Guide*, Routledge.

du Gay, P. (2000) *In Praise of Bureaucracy*, SAGE.

Early Education and Childcare Coalition (2024) *Rescue and Reform: A Manifesto to Transform Early Education and Childcare in England*, EECC. Available at: www.earlyeducationchildcare.org/manifesto

Early Years Alliance (2021) *Breaking Point: The Impact of Recruitment and Retention Challenges on the Early Years Sector in England*, Early Years Alliance. Available at: www.eyalliance.org.uk/breaking-point-impact-recruitment-and-retention-challenges-early-years-sector-england

Early Years Coalition (2021) *Birth to 5 Matters: Non-Statutory Guidance for the Early Years Foundation Stage*, Early Years Alliance. Available at: https://birthto5matters.org.uk/download-or-buy-a-copy

Eberle, T.S. (1995) 'Relational knowledge in organizational theory: an exploration into some of its implications', in D.-M. Hosking, H.P. Dachler and K.J. Gergen (eds) *Management and Organization: Relational Alternatives to Individualism*, Avebury, pp 201–19.

Edwards, M., Gatrell, C. and Sutton, A. (2023) 'The case for parentalism at work: balancing feminist care ethics and justice ethics through a Winnicottian approach: a school case study', *Journal of Business Ethics*, advance online publication. doi: 10.1007/s10551-023-05352-w

Einarsdottir, J. (2017) 'Opportunities and challenges in Icelandic early childhood education', in C. Ringsmose and G. Kragh-Muller (eds) *Nordic Social Pedagogical Approach to Early Years*, Springer, pp 63–72.

Elfer, P. (2007) 'What are nurseries for? The concept of primary task and its application in differentiating roles and tasks in nurseries', *Journal of Early Childhood Research*, 5(2): 169–88. doi: 10.1177/1476718X07076727

Elfer, P. (ed) (2024) *Talking with Feelings in the Early Years: 'Work Discussion' as a Model of Supporting Professional Reflection and Wellbeing*, Routledge.

Elkington, J. (1997) *Cannibals with Forks: The Triple Bottom Line of 21st Century Business*, Capstone Publishing.

Elley-Brown, M.J. and Pringle, J.K. (2019) 'Sorge, Heideggerian ethic of care: creating more caring organizations', *Journal of Business Ethics*, 168(1): 23–35. doi: 10.1007/s10551-019-04243-3

Enright, A. (2004) *Making Babies: Stumbling into Motherhood*, Norton.

Ferguson, K.E. (1984) *The Feminist Case against Bureaucracy*, Temple.

Field, T. (2010) 'Touch for socioemotional and physical well-being: a review', *Developmental Review*, 30(4): 367–83. doi: 10.1016/j.dr.2011.01.001

Fine, C. (2010) *Delusions of Gender*, Icon.

Fine, C. (2017) *Testosterone Rex*, Icon.

Fisher, B. and Tronto, J. (1990) 'Toward a feminist theory of caring', in E.K. Abel and M.K. Nelson (eds) *Circles of Care: Work and Identity in Women's Lives*, State University of New York Press, pp 35–62.

Furedi, F. (2001) *Paranoid Parenting: Abandon Your Anxieties and be a Good Parent*, Allen Lane.

Gallagher, A. (2017) 'Growing pains? Change in the New Zealand childcare market 2006-2016', *New Zealand Geographer*, 73(1): 1–12. doi: 10.1111/nzg.12147

Gehman, J., Treviño, L.K. and Garud, R. (2013) 'Values work: a process study of the emergence and performance of organizational values practices', *Academy of Management Journal*, 56(1): 84–112. doi: 10.5465/amj.2010.0628

Georgeson, J. (2009) 'Co-constructing meaning: differences in the interactional micro-climate', in T. Papatheodorou and J. Moyles (eds) *Learning Together in the Early Years: Exploring Relational Pedagogy*, Routledge, pp 109–19.

Gerhardt, S. (2004) *Why Love Matters*, Brunner-Routledge.

Gherardi, S. (2012) *How to Conduct a Practice-Based Study*, Edward Elgar.

Gherardi, S. and Rodeschini, G. (2016) 'Caring as a collective knowledgeable doing: about concern and being concerned', *Management Learning*, 47(3): 266–84. doi: 10.1177/1350507615610030

Gill, T. (2007) *No Fear: Growing Up in a Risk Averse Society*, Calouste Gulbenkian Foundation.

Gilligan, C. (1982) *In a Different Voice*, Harvard University Press.

Gilligan, C. and Snider, N. (2018) *Why Does Patriarchy Persist?* Polity Press.

Gioia, D.A. and Chittipeddi, K. (1991) 'Sensemaking and sensegiving in strategic change initiation', *Strategic Management Journal*, 12(6): 433–48. doi: 10.1002/smj.4250120604

Goldstein, L.S. (1998) 'More than gentle smiles and warm hugs: applying the ethic of care to early childhood education', *Journal of Research in Childhood Education*, 12(2): 244–61. doi: 10.1080/02568549809594888

Gopnik, A. (2016) *The Gardener and the Carpenter: What the New Science of Child Development Tells Us about the Relationship Between Parents and Children*, Vintage.

Granovetter, M. (1985) 'Economic action and social structure: the problem of embeddedness', *The American Journal of Sociology*, 91(3): 481–510. doi: 10.1086/228311

Hadjimichael, D. and Tsoukas, H. (2019) 'Towards a better understanding of tacit knowledge in organizations: taking stock and moving forward', *Academy of Management Annals*, 13(2). doi: 10.5465/annals.2017.0084

Hadjimichael, D., Pyrko, I. and Tsoukas, H. (2023) 'Beyond tacit knowledge: how Michael Polanyi's theory of knowledge illuminates theory development in organizational research', *Academy of Management Review*, advance online publication. doi: 10.5465/amr.2022.0289

Hamington, M. (2004) *Embodied Care: Jane Addams, Maurice Merleau-Ponty, and Feminist Ethics*, University of Illinois Press.

Hamington, M. (2015) 'Politics is not a game', in D. Engster and M. Hamington (eds) *Care Ethics & Political Theory*, Oxford University Press, pp 272–92.

Hardy, K., Tomlinson, J., Norman, H., Cruz, K., Whittaker, X. and Archer, N. (2022) *Essential but Undervalued: Early Years Care & Education during COVID-19*, University of Leeds. Available at: https://eyehub.leeds.ac.uk/cdc-19-final-report

Hardy, K., Stephens, L., Tomlinson, J., Valizade, D., Whittaker, X., Norman, H. and Moffat, R. (2024) *Retention and Return: Delivering the Expansion of Early Years Entitlement in England*, Early Education and Childcare Coalition. Available at: www.earlyeducationchildcare.org/early-years-workforce-report

Harlow, H.F., Dodsworth, R.O. and Harlow, M.K. (1965) 'Total social isolation in monkeys', *Psychology*, 54: 90–7.

Harter, J.K., Schmidt, F.L. and Keyes, C.L.M. (2003) 'Well-being in the workplace and its relationship to business outcomes: a review of the Gallup studies', in C.L.M. Keyes and J. Haidt (eds) *Flourishing: Positive Psychology and the Life Well-Lived*, American Psychological Association, pp 205–24.

Held, V. (1993) *Feminist Morality: Transforming Culture, Society, and Politics*, University of Chicago Press.

Held, V. (2006) *The Ethics of Care: Personal, Political, and Global*, Oxford University Press.

Hochschild, A.R. (2012) *The Managed Heart* (updated with a new preface), University of California Press.

Hooks, B. (2001) *All About Love: New Visions*, Harper Collins.

House of Commons Committee of Public Accounts (2016) *Entitlement to Free Early Years Education and Childcare: Fourth Report of Session 2016–17*, HC 224. Available at: https://publications.parliament.uk/pa/cm201617/cmselect/cmpubacc/224/224.pdf

House of Commons Education Committee (2019) *Tackling Disadvantage in the Early Years: Ninth Report of Session 2017–19*, HC 1006. Available at: https://publications.parliament.uk/pa/cm201719/cmselect/cmeduc/1006/1006.pdf

Howard, S.J., Siraj, I., Melhuish, E.C., Kingston, D., Neilsen-Hewett, C., de Rosnay, M. et al (2018) 'Measuring interactional quality in pre-school settings: introduction and validation of the Sustained Shared Thinking and Emotional Wellbeing (SSTEW) scale', *Early Child Development and Care*, 190(7): 1017–30. doi: 10.1080/03004430.2018.1511549

Isenbarger, L. and Zembylas, M. (2006) 'The emotional labour of caring in teaching', *Teaching and Teacher Education*, 22(1): 120–34. doi: 10.1016/j.tate.2005.07.002

Jarman, E. (2013) *The Communication-Friendly Spaces Approach*, Elizabeth Jarman Ltd.

Jarvis, P. (2020) 'Attachment theory, cortisol and care for the under-threes in the twenty-first century: constructing evidence-informed policy', *Early Years*, advance online publication. doi: 10.1080/09575146.2020.1764507

Jensen, J.J. (2011) 'Understandings of Danish pedagogical practice', in C. Cameron and P. Moss (eds) *Social Pedagogy and Working with Children and Young People: Where Care and Education Meet*, Jessica Kingsley Publishers, pp 141–57.

Jones, E.B. and Bartunek, J.M. (2021) 'Too close or optimally positioned? The value of personally relevant research', *Academy of Management Perspectives*, 35(3): 335–46. doi: 10.5465/AMP.2018.0009

Kahn, W.A. (1993) 'Caring for the caregivers: patterns of organizational caregiving', *Administrative Science Quarterly*, 38(4): 539–63. doi: 10.2307/2393336

Kingston-Hughes, B. (2022) *A Very Unusual Journey into Play*, SAGE.

Laevers, F. (1994) *The Leuven Involvement Scale for Young Children* [manual and video], Leuven.

Langford, R. (2019) *Theorizing Feminist Ethics of Care in Early Childhood Practice*, Bloomsbury.

Langford, R. and Richardson, B. (2020) 'Ethics of care in practice: an observational study of interactions and power relations between children and educators in urban Ontario early childhood settings', *Journal of Childhood Studies*, 45(1): 33–47. doi: 10.18357/jcs00019398

Lawrence, T.B. and Maitlis, S. (2012) 'Care and possibility: enacting an ethic of care through narrative practice', *Academy of Management Review*, 37(4): 641–63. doi: 10.5465/amr.2010.0466

Let Toys Be Toys (2021) *Who Gets to Play Now?* Let Toys Be Toys. Available at: https://app.box.com/s/qi3pdp5bh5yj4kadblyy13nml605yvbn

Lloyd, E. (2023) *A Public Good Approach: Learning from Ireland's Early Education and Childcare Reform*, Early Education and Childcare Coalition. Available at: www.earlyeducationchildcare.org/ireland-reforms

Lloyd, E. and Penn, H. (2013) *Childcare Markets: Can They Deliver an Equitable Service?* Policy Press.

Lloyd, E. and Potter, S. (2014) *Early Childhood Education and Care and Poverty*, Joseph Rowntree Foundation.

Louv, R. (2005) *Last Child in the Woods: Saving Our Children from Nature-Deficit Disorder*, Atlantic Books.

Louv, R. (2012) *The Nature Principle: Reconnecting with Life in a Virtual Age*, Algonquin Books.

Lucas, C. (2024) *Another England: How to Reclaim Our National Story*, Hutchinson Heinemann.

Mackenzie, C. and Stoljar, N. (2000) *Relational Autonomy*, Oxford University Press.

Maitlis, S. (2005) 'The social processes of organizational sensemaking', *Academy of Management Journal*, 48(1): 21–49. doi: 10.5465/amj.2005.15993111

Maitlis, S. and Lawrence, T.B. (2007) 'Triggers and enablers of sensegiving in organizations', *Academy of Management Journal*, 50(1): 57–84. doi: 10.5465/AMJ.2007.24160971

Maitlis, S. and Christianson, M. (2014) 'Sensemaking in organizations: taking stock and moving forward', *Academy of Management Annals*, 8(1): 57–125. doi: 10.1080/19416520.2014.873177

Maitlis, S., Vogus, T.J. and Lawrence, T.B. (2013) 'Sensemaking and emotion in organizations', *Organizational Psychology Review*, 3(3): 222–47. doi: 10.1177/2041386613489062

Manning-Morton, J. (2024) *From Birth to Three: An Early Years Educator's Handbook*, Routledge.

Martin, J.R. (1992) *The Schoolhome*, Harvard University Press.

Mathers, S., Ranns, H., Karemaker, A., Moody, A., Sylva, K., Graham, J. and Siraj-Blatchford, I. (2011) *Evaluation of the Graduate Leader Fund: Final Report*, Department for Health.

Mathers, S., Eisenstadt, N., Sylva, K., Soukakou, E. and Ereky-Stevens, K. (2014) *Sound Foundations: A Review of the Research Evidence on Quality of Early Childhood Education and Care for Children Under Three: Implications for Policy and Practice*, The Sutton Trust.

McGregor, D. (2006) *The Human Side of Enterprise* (annotated edn), McGraw-Hill.

McMillan, M. (1919) *The Nursery School*, Dent & Sons.

Melhuish, E. and Gardiner, J. (2018, revised 2021) *Study of Early Education and Development (SEED): Impact Study on Early Education Use and Child Outcomes Up to Age Four Years. Research Report*, NatCen Social Research, University of Oxford, and Action for Children.

Melhuish, E. and Gardiner, J. (2019) 'Structural factors and policy change as related to the quality of early childhood education and care for 3–4 year olds in the UK', *Frontiers in Education*, 4: art 35. doi: 10.3389/feduc.2019.00035

Montagu, A. (1986) *Touching: The Human Significance of the Skin* (3rd edn), Perennial.

Montessori, M. (1912) *The Montessori Method: Scientific Pedagogy as Applied to Child Education in 'The Children's Houses' with Additions and Revisions by the Author*, Frederick A. Stokes.

Montessori, M. (1948) *The Discovery of the Child*, Kalakshetra.

Moss, P. (2023) 'Introduction: from the politically impossible to the politically inevitable', in M. Vandenbroeck, J. Lehrer and L. Mitchell (eds) *The Decommodification of Early Childhood Education and Care*, Routledge, pp 1–14.

Moss, P. and Mitchell, L. (2024) *Early Childhood in the Anglosphere*, UCL Press.

Murray, C.G. (2021) *Illuminating Care: The Pedagogy and Practice of Care in Early Childhood Communities*, Exchange Press.

Music, G. (2017) *Nurturing Natures*, Routledge.

Noddings, N. (2002) *Starting at Home: Caring and Social Policy*, University of California Press.

Noddings, N. (2010a) 'Complexity in caring and empathy', *Abstracta*, 5(Suppl 5): 6–12.

Noddings, N. (2010b) *The Maternal Factor*, University of California Press.

Noddings, N. (2013) *Caring: A Relational Approach to Ethics and Moral Education* (2nd edn, updated), University of California Press.

Noddings, N. (2015) 'Care ethics and "caring" organizations', in D. Engster and M. Hamington (eds) *Care Ethics & Political Theory*, Oxford University Press, pp 72–84.

Nonaka, I. and Takeuchi, H. (1995) *The Knowledge-Creating Company*, Oxford University Press.

Norman, A. (2019) *From Conception to Two Years: Development, Policy and Practice*, Routledge.

Nuffield Trust (2024) 'Breastfeeding', *Nuffield Trust*, last updated 31 October. Available at: www.nuffieldtrust.org.uk/resource/breastfeeding

Nutbrown, C. (2012) *Foundation for Quality: The Independent Review of Early Education and Childcare Qualifications. Final Report*, Department for Education. Available at: www.gov.uk/government/publications/nutbrown-review-foundations-for-quality

OECD (Organisation for Economic Co-operation and Development) (2006) *Starting Strong II: Early Childhood Education and Care*, OECD.

OECD (Organisation for Economic Co-operation and Development) (2025) *Reducing Inequalities by Investing in Early Childhood Education and Care*, OECD.

Ofsted (2021) 'How early years multiple providers work', *GOV.UK*. Available at: www.gov.uk/government/publications/how-early-years-multiple-providers-work/how-early-years-multiple-providers-work

Oppenheim, C. and Milton, C. (2021) *3: Changing Patterns of Poverty in Early Childhood: The Changing Face of Early Childhood in the UK*, Nuffield Foundation.

Osgood, J. (2010) 'Reconstructing professionalism in ECEC: the case for the "critically reflective emotional professional"', *Early Years*, 30(2): 119–33. doi: 10.1080/09575146.2010.490905

Page, J. (2018) 'Characterising the principles of Professional Love in early childhood care and education', *International Journal of Early Years Education*, 26(2): 125–41. doi: 10.1080/09669760.2018.1459508

Page, J., Clare, A. and Nutbrown, C. (2013) *Working with Babies and Children from Birth to Three* (2nd edn), SAGE.

Papatheodorou, T. (2009) 'Exploring relational pedagogy', in T. Papatheodorou and J. Moyles (eds) *Learning Together in the Early Years: Exploring Relational Pedagogy*, Routledge, pp 3–17.

Parra Jounou, I. and Tronto, J.C. (2024) 'Care ethics in theory and practice: Joan C. Tronto in conversation with Iris Parra Jounou', *Contemporary Political Theory*, 23(2): 269–83. doi: 10.1057/s41296-024-00680-6

Paterson, M. (2007) *The Senses of Touch*, Berg.

Peeters, J. (2013) 'Towards a gender neutral interpretation of professionalism', *Revista Española de Educación Comparada*, 21: 119–44. doi: 10.5944/reec.21.2013.7617

Penn, H. (2011) 'Gambling on the market: the role of for-profit provision in early childhood education and care', *Journal of Early Childhood Research*, 9(2): 150–61. doi: 10.1177/1476718X103879

Penn, H. (2012) 'Childcare markets: do they work?', in E. Lloyd and H. Penn (eds) *Childcare Markets: Can They Deliver an Equitable Service?* Policy Press, pp 19–42.

Penn, H. (2017) 'Anything to divert attention from poverty', in M. Vandenbroeck (ed) *Constructions of Neuroscience in Early Childhood Education*, Routledge, pp 54–67.

Penn, H. (2019) *'Be Realistic, Demand the Impossible': A Memoir of Work in Childcare and Education*, Routledge.

Penn, H. (2024) *Who Needs Nurseries? We Do!* Policy Press.

Polanyi, M. (1958) *Personal Knowledge*, University of Chicago Press.

Pregnant Then Screwed (2022) '6 in 10 women who have had an abortion claim childcare costs influenced their decision', *Pregnant Then Screwed*, 8 July. Available at: https://pregnantthenscrewed.com/6-in-10-women-who-have-had-an-abortion-claim-childcare-costs-influenced-their-decision

Puig de la Bellacasa, M. (2017) *Matters of Care*, University of Minnesota Press.

Purvis, B., Mao, Y. and Robinson, D. (2019) 'Three pillars of sustainability: in search of conceptual origins', *Sustainability Science*, 14: 681–95. doi: 10.1007/s11625-018-0627-5

Raworth, K. (2017) *Doughnut Economics: Seven Ways to Think Like a 21st-Century Economist*, Chelsea Green.

Reed, J. (2025) *Social Enterprise and the Future of Early Years Provision in the UK*, Isos Partnership.

Reed, J. and O'Halloran, J. (2024) *The Childcare Challenge: How Can the New Government Deliver a Real Childcare Guarantee*, IPPR. Available at: www.ippr.org/articles/the-childcare-challenge

Richardson, B., Powell, A. and Langford, R. (2021) 'Critiquing Ontario's childcare policy responses to the inextricably connected needs of mothers, children, and early childhood educators', *Journal of Childhood Studies*, 46(3): 3–15. doi: 10.18357/jcs463202119951

Riley-Smith, B. (2021) 'Childcare rules will be relaxed to lower childcare costs for parents', *The Daily Telegraph*, 1 October. Available at: www.telegraph.co.uk/politics/2021/10/01/exclusive-childcare-rules-will-relaxed-lower-costs

Rippon, G. (2019) *The Gendered Brain*, The Bodley Head.

Roberts-Holmes, G. and Moss, P. (2021) *Neoliberalism and Early Childhood Education*, Routledge.

Rosen, R. (2019) 'Care as ethic, care as labor', in R. Langford (ed) *Theorizing Feminist Ethics of Care in Early Childhood Practice: Possibilities and Dangers*, Bloomsbury, pp 79–96.

Ruddick, S. (1980) 'Maternal thinking', *Feminist Studies*, 6(2): 342–67. doi: 10.2307/3177749

Ruddick, S. (1989) *Maternal Thinking: Towards a Politics of Peace*, The Women's Press.

Ruddick, S. (1998) 'Care as labor and relationship', in J.G. Haber and M.S. Halfon (eds) *Norms and Values: Essays on the Work of Virginia Held*, Rowan & Littlefield, pp 3–25.

Ruddick, S. (2009) 'On *Maternal Thinking*', *Women's Studies Quarterly*, 37(3/4): 305–8.

Saini, A. (2017) *Inferior*, 4th Estate.

Sandberg, J. and Tsoukas, H. (2015) 'Making sense of the sensemaking perspective: its constituents, limitations, and opportunities for further development', *Journal of Organizational Behavior*, 36: 6–32. doi: 10.1002/job.1937

Sandberg, J. and Tsoukas, H. (2020) 'Sensemaking reconsidered: towards a broader understanding through phenomenology', *Organization Theory*, 1(1). doi: 10.1177/2631787719879937

Sandseter, E.B.H. (2009) 'Children's expressions of exhilaration and fear in risky play', *Contemporary Issues in Early Childhood*, 10(2): 92–106. doi: 10.2304/ciec.2009.10.2.92

Sandseter, E.B.H. and Lysklett, O.B. (2017) 'Outdoor education in the Nordic region', in C. Ringsmose and G. Kragh-Muller (eds) *Nordic Social Pedagogical Approach to Early Years*, Springer, pp 115–32.

Save the Children (2018) *Lost Opportunities, Lost Incomes*, Save the Children. Available at: https://resourcecentre.savethechildren.net/pdf/lost-opportunities-lost-incomes.pdf

Schon, D.A. (1983) *The Reflective Practitioner*, Basic.

Scudellari, M. (2017) 'Cleaning up the hygiene hypothesis', *Proceedings of the National Academy of Sciences of the United States of America*, 114(7): 1433–6. doi: 10.1073/pnas.1700688114

Segal, L. (2023) *Lean on Me: A Politics of Radical Care*, Verso.

Seigfried, C.H. (1996) *Pragmatism and Feminism*, University of Chicago Press.

Sevilla, A. and Smith, S. (2020) 'Baby steps: the gender division of childcare during the COVID-19 pandemic', *Oxford Review of Economic Policy*, 36(Suppl 1): S169–S186. doi: 10.1093/oxrep/graa027

Shotter, J. and Cunliffe, A.L. (2003) 'Managers as practical authors: everyday conversations for action', in D. Holman and R. Thorpe (eds) *Management and Language: The Manager as a Practical Author*, SAGE, pp 15–37.

Simola, S. (2012) 'Exploring "embodied care" in relation to social sustainability', *Journal of Business Ethics*, 107(4): 473–84. doi: 10.1007/s10551-011-1059-7

Simon, A., Penn, H., Shah, A., Owen, C., Lloyd, E., Hollingworth, K. et al (2022) *Acquisitions, Mergers and Debt: The New Language of Childcare*, UCL Social Research Institute, University College London.

Simpson, D., Lumsden, E. and McDowall Clark, R. (2015) 'Neoliberalism, global poverty policy and early childhood education and care: a critique of local uptake in England', *Early Years*, 35(1): 96–109. doi: 10.1080/09575146.2014.969199

Sims, M. (2014) 'Is the care–education dichotomy behind us? Should it be?', *Australasian Journal of Early Childhood*, 39(4): 4–11. doi: 10.1177/183693911403900402

Siraj-Blatchford, I. (2009) 'Conceptualising progression in the pedagogy of play and sustained shared thinking in early childhood education: a Vygotskian perspective', *Educational and Child Psychology*, 26(2): 77–89. doi: 10.53841/bpsecp.2009.26.2.77

Slote, M. (2007) *The Ethics of Care and Empathy*, Routledge.

Slow Food in the UK (nd) Home page. Available at: www.slowfood.org.uk

Sonenshein, S. (2007) 'The role of construction, intuition, and justification in responding to ethical issues at work: the sensemaking-intuition model', *Academy of Management Review*, 32(4): 1022–40. doi: 10.5465/AMR.2007.26585677

Spock, B. and Parker, S.J. (1998) *Dr Spock's Baby and Child Care*, Simon & Schuster.

Statham, R., Freedman, S. and Parkes, H. (2022) *Delivering a Childcare Guarantee*, IPPR. Available at: www.ippr.org/articles/delivering-a-childcare-guarantee

Steedman, C. (1985) '"The mother made conscious": the historical development of a primary school pedagogy', *History Workshop Journal*, 20(1): 149–63. doi: 10.1093/hwj/20.1.149

Strati, A. (2007) 'Sensible knowledge and practice-based learning', *Management Learning*, 38(1): 61–77. doi: 10.1177/1350507607073023

Sumsion, J. (2013) 'ABC Learning and Australian early education and care: a retrospective ethical audit of a radical experiment', in E. Lloyd and H. Penn (eds) *Childcare Markets: Can They Deliver an Equitable Service?* Policy Press, pp 209–25.

Sylva, K., Melhuish, E., Sammons, P., Siraj-Blatchford, I. and Taggart, B. (2004) *The Effective Provision of Pre-School Education [EPPE] Project. Technical Paper 12: The Final Report: Effective Pre-School Education*, Institute of Education. Available at: http://discovery.ucl.ac.uk/10005308/1/EPPE12Sylva2004Effective.pdf

Taggart, G. (2011) 'Don't we care? The ethics and emotional labour of early years professionalism', *Early Years*, 31(1): 85–95. doi: 10.1080/09575146.2010.536948

Taggart, G. (2019) 'Cultivating ethical dispositions in early childhood practice for an ethic of care: a contemplative approach', in R. Langford (ed) *Theorizing Feminist Ethics of Care in Early Chilidhood Practice: Possibilities and Dangers*, Bloomsbury, pp 97–123.

Tickell, C. (2011) *The Early Years: Foundations For Life, Health And Learning*, Department for Education. Available at: www.gov.uk/government/publications/the-early-years-foundations-for-life-health-and-learning-an-independent-report-on-the-early-years-foundation-stage-to-her-majestys-government

Tomkins, L. and Simpson, P. (2015) 'Caring leadership: a Heideggerian perspective', *Organization Studies*, 36(8): 1013–31. doi: 10.1177/0170840615580008

Trevino, L.K. (1986) 'Ethical decision making in organizations: a person-situation interactionist model', *Academy of Management Review*, 11(3): 601–17. doi: 10.5465/AMR.1986.4306235

Tronto, J.C. (1993) *Moral Boundaries: A Political Argument for an Ethic of Care*, Routledge.

Tronto, J.C. (2010) 'Creating caring institutions: politics, plurality, and purpose', *Ethics and Social Welfare*, 4(2): 158–71. doi: 10.1080/17496535.2010.484259

Tronto, J.C. (2013) *Caring Democracy: Markets, Equality and Justice*, New York University Press.

Tsoukas, H. (2002) 'Do we really understand tacit knowledge?', in M. Easterby-Smith and M. Lyles (eds) *Handbook of Organizational Learning and Knowledge*, Blackwell, pp 410–27.

Uhl-Bien, M. (2006) 'Relational leadership theory: exploring the social processes of leadership and organizing', *Leadership Quarterly*, 17(6): 654–76. doi: 10.1016/j.leaqua.2006.10.007

United Nations (1989) Convention on the Rights of the Child, Treaty no 27531, United Nations Treaty Series 3–178.

Vandenbroeck, M., Lehrer, J. and Mitchell, L. (2023) 'Resisting the consumentality of parents', in M. Vandenbroeck, J. Lehrer and L. Mitchell (eds) *The Decommodification of Early Childhood Education and Care*, Routledge, pp 81–146.

Van Laere, K., Peeters, J. and Vandenbroeck, M. (2012) 'The education and care divide: the role of the early childhood workforce in 15 European countries', *European Journal of Education*, 47(4): 527–41. doi: 10.1111/ejed.12006

Van Laere, K., Vandenbroeck, M., Roets, G. and Peeters, J. (2014) 'Challenging the feminisation of the workforce: rethinking the mind-body dualism in early childhood education and care', *Gender and Education*, 26(3): 232–45. doi: 10.1080/09540253.2014.901721

Van Laere, K., Roets, G. and Vandenbroeck, M. (2019) 'The controversy of Ravza's pacifier: in search of embodied care in preschool education', in R. Langford (ed) *Theorizing Feminist Ethics of Care in Early Childhood Practice: Possibilities and Dangers*, Bloomsbury, pp 163–84.

Vygotsky, L.S. (1978) *Mind in Society*, Harvard University Press.

Weick, K.E. (1995) *Sensemaking in Organizations*, SAGE.

Weick, K.E. (2012) 'Organized sensemaking: a commentary on processes of interpretive work', *Human Relations*, 65(1): 141–53. doi: 10.1177/0018726711424235

Whipps, J.D. (2012) 'Feminist-pragmatist democratic practice and contemporary sustainability movements', in M. Hamington and C. Bardwell-Jones (eds) *Contemporary Feminist Pragmatism*, Routledge, pp 115–27.

Williams, F. (2001) 'In and beyond New Labour: towards a new political ethics of care', *Critical Social Policy*, 21(4): 467–93. doi: 10.1177/026101830102100405

Williams, F. (2018) 'Care: intersections of scales, inequalities and crises', *Current Sociology*, 66(4): 547–61. doi: 10.1177/0011392118765206

Winnicott, D. (1971) *Playing and Reality*, Routledge.

World Health Organization (2023) 'Infant and young child feeding', *World Health Organization*, 20 December. Available at: www.who.int/news-room/fact-sheets/detail/infant-and-young-child-feeding

Wuori, D. (2024) *The Daycare Myth: What We Get Wrong about Early Care and Education (and What We Should Do about It)*, Teachers College Press.

Zeedyk, S. (2006) 'From intersubjectivity to subjectivity: the transformative roles of emotional intimacy and imitation', *Infant and Child Development*, 44(15): 321–44. doi: 10.1002/icd.457

Zeedyk, S. (2008) *What's Life in a Baby Buggy Like? The Impact of Buggy Orientation on Parent-Infant Interaction and Infant Stress*, University of Dundee.

Zeedyk, S. (2014) 'How buggies shape babies' brains', *Suzanne Zeedyk*, 3 April. Available at: https://suzannezeedyk.com/how-buggies-shape-babies-brains

Zeedyk, S. (nd) 'Tigers & Teddies Nursery series – partings and reunions', *connected baby*. Available at: https://suzannezeedyk.com/portfolio/tigers-teddies-nursery-series-partings-reunions

Index

References to figures appear in *italic* type; those in **bold** type refer to tables.

A

ABC Learning 114–15
abortions 17
absorbed coping 94
'acaring' (Hamington) 39–40
'accelerated childhood' 78
Acorn Early Years Foundation 3, 11, 18, 22, 26
Addams, Jane 68
additional needs children 23
adult-directed learning 59
affectionate touching 62
'affinity to children' 28
affordability of childcare 2, 25
age range of 'early years' 6
Ahmed, Sara 81
Ailwood, J. 46
alert to dangers 77–8
All-Party Parliamentary Group on a Fit and Healthy Childhood 63, 75
Anglosphere 29–30
attachment theory (J. Bowlby) 57–8
attentiveness 58, 64–5
Australia 29
autonomy and agency 105

B

'Baby Lab' experiments 108
baby rooms 83
behaviourist approaches 63
Bell, D.C. 57–8
best practice 6, 27
Birth to 5 Matters guidance (Early Years Coalition) 10
Birth to Three Matters framework 4
Blair/Brown Labour government 25, 27
boarding schools 55
Bone, J. 80
bottle-feeding 64, 72, 83
boundary objects 81, 87
Bowden, Peta 39, **50**
Bowlby, J. 57
breastfeeding 71–4
Bregman, Rutger 9, 108
Bright Horizons 21
buggies 81–2
bureaucracy 37
Byron, Tanya 63

C

camaraderie and friendships 108
Canada 29, 51
care
  as a buzzword 53
  defining 6–7
  dimension of love 76
  as a moral theory 53
  negative connotations 50
  organisational competence 33, 55
Care Collective 2, 7, 55
care ethics 46–61, 112
  early years practice 53–4
  entrepreneurial process 37, **38**
  gender 50–3
  maternalism 46–7
  organising principle 54–7
  relational approaches 47–9
  relational pedagogy 57–8
  sustainability 113–14
caregiving 56, 57–8, 118
The Care Manifesto (Chatzidakis) 2, 7, 55
care manifesto (Raven) 119–20
'care-receiving' (Tronto) 56, 118
care routines 59–60, 63–4
carewashing 33, *95*, 115
'caring about' (Tronto) 55, 118
caring dispositions 120
caring employment practices 55
caring for caregivers 33–5
'caring habits' (Hamington) 68, *68*, 69–70, *109*, 110, 117
'caring imagination' (Hamington) 67, *68*, *109*, 110–11, 117
'caring knowledge' (Hamington) 67, *68*, 109–10, *109*, 117
caring leadership 54
Caring (Noddings) 48
caring relations 48–9
'caring with' (Tronto) 56, 114, 118
Central European countries 30
chairs 80, 82–4
charity-run nursery models 18, 115
Chatzidakis, A. 2, 7, 33, 55
childcare
  public understanding 2, 23–4
  use of term 5–7, 30
  and working families 53
child-led learning 88

135

children
  crying and distressed 39, 44, 68, 75–6
  dressing appropriately 78
  emotional attachments 74
  emotional needs 76
  individual needs 24, 65
  self-regulation 76
  understanding ethnicities 108
children of colour 86
Chodorow, Nancy **50**
Clark, Alison 78
climate crisis 117–18
clothing 78, 84–6
Cloyes, K.G. 50
Coalition government 27
commodification of childcare 4, 10, 19, 112
consumer 10, 19, 74
contested terms 4–5
continuing professional development (CPD) 26
Convention on the Rights of a Child (United Nations) 10
'conviviality' (Polanyi) 71
cortisol 58
cost of childcare 16–17
COVID-19 pandemic 82
  morale 24
  online interviews 12
  parental roles 51–2
  PPE 84
  social distancing 35, 63, 111
critical reflection 67
cuddling 62, 68–9
Cunliffe, A.L. 106
Cutting, K. 103–4

D

'day care' 7
The Daycare Myth (Wuori) 31–2
day nurseries 6, 21, 78–9
decision-making 100–3
Delivering a Childcare Guarantee (Statham/IPPR) 39
demand-side funding 19
demand without supply 31
Denmark 8, 59
Department for Education (DfE) 57, 60
deprivation funding 23
desks 80
detached-deliberate sensemaking 95, **96–7**, 99
Dewey, John 61, **61**, 93, 110
dialogical opportunities 106–7
Diderot, Denis 65
disadvantaged families and children 16, 23
'Doughnut Economics' model (Raworth) 115–16

E

'early care and education' (Raven) 8
early childhood care and education (ECCE) 3, 6, 16
'early childhood education' (Moss) 7
Early Education and Childcare Coalition 7, 16
'early years' 5, 6
Early Years Alliance 5, 24
Early Years and Childcare Coalition 26
Early Years Coalition 10
Early Years Educator qualification 5
Early Years Foundation Stage framework (DfE) 4, 8, 10, 57, 60
early years practice 6, 53–4
early years professionals 4–5, 9, 25, 83–4
early years settings 116–17
  see also nurseries
Early Years Teacher Status 4
early years theorists 60–1, **61**
early years workforce 51–3
economic well-being 16–17
education 7–10
Effective Provision of Pre-School Education Project (Sylva) 60
Einarsdottir, J. 25, 30
Elfer, P. 9
embedded ethical sensemaking 95
embedded ethic of care 119
embodied and sensory learning 47
embodied care (Hamington) 67–8, *68*, 109–10, *109*, 117
embodied ethical sensemaking 108–11, *109*, 113
embodied perception (Hamington) 70
emergency childcare 21
emotional attachments 74
emotional impacts of objects 81
emotional labour (Hochschild) 33–4, 74–5
'emotional stickiness' (Gallagher) 20, 74
emotions in childcare practice 74–6
empathy 49, 67
engrossment (Noddings) 110
Enright, Anne 73
entrepreneurial processes 37–9, **38**
environmental sustainability 117–18
equal parenting 2
'ethical caring' (Noddings) 49–50, 67, 108, 113
ethical childcare 54
ethical decision-making 100, 102, 105, 108
ethical sensegiving 93–4, *95*, 99, 106–8
ethical sensemaking 93–111
  and decision-making 100–3, 108
  and embodied practice 108–9, *109*
  organisational learning 106
  reflective practice 119

and relationships 102–3
and sensegiving 106–8
see also sensemaking
ethical slippage 39–43, 103–6
ethics of care 2, 7, 10, 53–4, 117
ethics of care theorists 49–50, **50**
experiential knowledge 118
explicit knowledge 66

F

faking cheerfulness 74–5
fast foods 117
fathering 4, 50–1
feedback loops 56
feeling cared for 35
feminine traits 51
feminist ethic of care 24, 45, 55
feminist theory of care 117
financial sustainability 43, 114–15
Fine, C. 51
Fisher, Bernice 6, 78, 117
Ford, Gina 63
forest schools 18, 92
four phases of care (Tronto) 37, 55–6, 117–18
fragmented ethical sensemaking *95*, 108
France 30
Frederick II, emperor of Germany 62
'free' 30-hours childcare 5, 16–17, 21–2, 41, 105
free market economics 19
free nursery meals 5, 41, 106
Froebel, Friedrich 46, 60, **61**
'full-time mothering ideological norm' (Chodorow) 51
functional and pleasant touching 63
funding issues 5, 11, 17, 21–3, 31
Furedi, Frank 75

G

Gallagher, A. 20, 74
Gallup Workforce Audit 35
Gardiner, J. 60
Gehman, J. 98
gender issues 4, 6, 25, 50–3
gender-neutrality 45, 52
gender stereotypes 48, 51
'get used to it' misconception 55
Gherardi, S. 33
Gilligan, Carol 48, **50**
Goldstein, L.S. 24
'good-enough mother' (Winnicott) 51
Gopnik, Alison 10, 58
Graduate Leader Fund 27, 30
graduate leaders 8–9, 25, 27, 29
graduate qualifications 4, 8, 25, 27–8
Green, Christopher 63

green spaces 91
'grey' literature 13

H

habitual behaviours 39, 110
Hadjimichael, D. 70
Hamington, Maurice 39, **50**, 67–70, *68*, 109, 110, 117
Harlow, H.F. 62
Held, Virginia **50**, 74
highly leveraged financial models 115
high-quality care and education 1, 16, 69–70
Hochschild, A.R. 33
holistic approaches 4, 30
hooks, bel (Gloria Watkins) 76
'How early years multiple providers work' (Ofsted) 36–7
Humankind (Bregman) 108

I

Iceland 25, 30, 101–2
ideal of family life 33
immanent sensemaking 94, **96–7**
inclusion 115–17
independence 55
inductive approaches 12
'indwelling' (Hadjimichael and Tsoukas) 70, 71
inequalities 16, 115
instinctive behaviour 49
Institute for Public Policy Research (IPPR) 22, 38–9
interviews 12–14
intuition ('gut instinct') 54–5, 97
involved-deliberate sensemaking 95, **96–7**, 99
Ireland 25, 32

J

James, William 93
Jarman, Elizabeth 81
Jarvis, P. 58
Jensen, Jytte Juul 59
justice-based approach to ethics 24, 45

K

key performance indicators (KPIs) 35–6, 44
key person approaches 40, 57–8, 64
kindergarten movement 46
King, Frederic Truby (Truby King) 63, 66, 76
knowledge and skills 118
knowledge creation models 66
kropsglighed 8, 59

L

Laevers, F. 65
language and sensemaking 93

leadership 41, 43–5, 119
learning
  best practice examples 31
  and development 25–9
  as reflective/reflexive dialogue 106
left-handed children 86–7
Let Toys Be Toys 52, 88, *89*
'levels of involvement' (Leuven Scale) 65
'limpet theory' (Penn) 58
listening 77
litter-picking activities 91
Lloyd, Eva 16, 20, 32
local authority nurseries 20
Louv, Richard 18, 91, 118
'love ethic' (hooks) 76
low-income families 16, 23
Lucas, Caroline 91

M

maintained nursery schools 4, 19, 23, 38
Maitlis, Sally 94
Malaguzzi, Loris **61**
male and female voices 48
managers 34–7, 43–4, 119
Manning-Morton, J. 62
marketisation 16–32, 112
  Anglosphere 29–30
  early years sector 19–21
  nurseries and schools 23
  professional development 27
  as a wrong turn 4
Martin, Jane Roland 33
'masculine' ethic of justice 45
material objects 80–4
material resources 118
maternal consciousness 48–9
maternalism 46–7, 112
maternity leave 2, 71
Mathers, S. 29
matrons 4–5
mature students 29
McMillan, Margaret 25, **61**, 89–90
Mead, George Herbert 93
mealtimes 17, 59, 80
Melhuish, E. 24, 60
men as carers 52–3
Merleau-Ponty, Maurice 67, 70
messy activities 88
micro resistances 100
minimal ethical sensemaking *95*
Mitchell, Linda 2, 30
mobile phones and tablets 82
Montagu, A. 63, 82
Montessori, Maria 46, 60, **61**, 80, 118
morale 24
'moral marketing gloss' (Puig de la Bellacasa) 33
Moss, Peter 2, 7, 30, 74

mother–child dyad 58
mothering 4, 46, 51
mothers
  idealisation 46
  returning to work 18, 53, 73
'motivational displacement' (Noddings) 57
Murray, Carol Garboden 7, 62
Music, G. 69

N

nappy changing 63, 64
National Minimum Wage 28
National Nursery Examination Board qualification (NNEB) 4, 84
'natural' caring (Noddings) 48–9, 50, 67
'nature deficit disorder' (Louv) 18, 91
neoliberalism 10, 19
new managerialism 24
New Zealand 29
Noddings, Nel 33, 48–50, **50**, 57, 67, 108, 110
Nonaka, I. 66
non-gendered play 88
non-working families 17
Nordic countries 8, 30, 90
nose blowing and wiping 59, 63, 85, 107
not-for-profit nurseries 37, 38
Nuffield Trust 71
nurseries
  caring culture 41
  communication 37–8
  cost of 'extras' 22
  decor 81, 87
  impact of large chains 32
  inspections 3–4
  pace of routines 77
  quality of childcare 81
  resources in poor condition 88
  sizes and on different floors 41–2
  supporting parents 23
  undervalued 34–5
  working hours 3, 21
nursery gardens 90
'nursery nurses' (NNEB) 4
'nursery nursing' 4–5
The Nursery School (McMillan) 89–90

O

occupancy targets 36
OECD 1, 3, 8, 19, 21
Ofsted 1, 3, 13, 36–7
O'Halloran, J. 22, 38
'one-caring' (Noddings) 49
open-air nursery schools 90
organisational sensemaking 94, *95*
organisations 33–45
  caring ethos 33
  culture and leadership 43–5

ethic of care 54–7
ethos and values 36–7
KPIs 35–6
leaders and managers 34–7, 43–4, 119
occupancy targets 36
ownership and governance 38
sizes 44
stories 93–4
O'Sullivan, June 9
outdoor clothing 84, 85–6
outdoor play and learning 30, 42–3, 89–92
oxytocin 68–9

P

pace 77, 79, 117, 120
Page, J. 58, 75, 76
'parentalist' ethic of care 45
parents
 as consumers 20
 'dropping off' and 'picking up' 5
 emotional needs 76
 gendered roles 51
 instructions on children's needs 104
 learning care technique 68
 partnership with carers 119
 selecting nurseries 1
 working 2, 20–1, 53, 55
part-time places 3, 21
paternity leave 2
Paterson, M. 65
pay-as-you-go private market 17
Peacock, S. 103–4
'pedagogues' and 'pedagogy' 4–5, 9
peer observations 66
Penn, Helen 20, 21, 58
performative professionalism 75
personal moral codes 98
personal protective equipment (PPE) 84–5
phenomenological arguments 67
phenomenology of care 57
Piaget, Jean 10, 48, 60, **61**
picking-up children 76–7
plants and animals 91
plastic gloves 64, 84–5
play and play facilities 9–10, 42–3, 86–8
Polanyi, M. 71
politicians 119
post-lunch routines 77
poverty 18–19
power relations 74
'practice' 6–7
practice-based approaches 33
practice theory 56–7
practitioner autonomy 103–6
pragmatist approaches 93
Pregnant Then Screwed (charity) 16–17
Pre-School Learning Alliance *see* Early Years Alliance

private equity 31–2
professional development 26, 27, 29
professional identity 105
professionalisation 46–7, 75
professional isolation 30
'professional love' (Page) 58, 75, 76
profits and profitability 19–20, 27, 35–7, 43, 115
protective clothing 84–6
Puig de la Bellacasa, María 33

Q

qualifications 2, 8, 25, 27–9, 30
quality of care 43, 60
quality of early education 29
quality, definition of 1

R

"rationality of care" (Ruddick) 47
Raven, Zoë 8, 120
Raworth, K. 115–16
'readiness for school' approaches 30
reciprocity from 'cared-for' (Noddings) 49
Reed, J. 22, 38
'reflection-in-action' (Schon) 94–5
reflective practice 93, 94, 119
relational approaches 11, 48–9, 53
relational pedagogies 45, 57–8, 60
relationships 102–3
representational sensemaking 95, **96–7**
research 11–14
respectful care 76–7, 99–100
restricted ethical sensemaking *95*
Richard, A.J 57–8
'risky play' 27
Rodeschini, G. 33
role models 54, 119–20
Ruddick, Sara 47–8, 50–1, **50**
rugs and cushions 81

S

salaries 19, 22–3
Sandberg, J. 94, 95, **96–7**, 110–11
sandboxes/sandpits/sand play 91
Save the Children 22, 38
Schon, D.A. 94
school bears 87
'schoolhome' model (Martin) 33
schoolification 2, 3, 7–10, 112
'school-readiness' 3, 8, 47
scissors 86–7
secure attachment relationships 57, 69
Segal, L. 21
sensegiving 93–100, *95*, 106–8
sensemaking 14, 93–8, *95*, **96–7**, 101–2
 see also ethical sensemaking
sensemaking-intuition model (SIM) 102–3
sessional early years education 6

settling-in process 78
short-term investment decisions 19
Shotter, J. 106
Simon, A. 32, 115
Simpson, P. 54
Sims, M. 9
single-use gloves 64, 84–5
skin-to-skin sensory experience 63
sleep-times 59–60, 63, 104
Slote, Michael 49
slow food movement 117
slow pedagogy 60
snack times 18
Snider, N. 48
social acceptability 47
social constructionism 11
social distancing 35, 63, 111
social engineering 51
social enterprises 18, 37–9, 115
social foundations 116
social interactions 83
social justice 17
social mobility 16
social pedagogy 30
social processes 93
social sustainability 115–17
sociomateriality 66, 80–2, 112
soft furnishings 82–4
Sonenshein, S. 102–3
songs and rhymes 71
special educational needs and disabilities (SEND) 116
Spock, Benjamin 66
staff rooms 83–4
staff-to-child ratios 22, 24, 31, 58, 77, 83
stages of development (Piaget) 60
Starting Strong report (OECD) 21
Statham, R. 39
Steedman, Carolyn 46
Steiner, Rudolf **61**
'still face' experiment (Tronick) 65
stools 80–1
storytelling 70–1
Strati, A. 85
stress and depression 63
Study of Early Education and Development (Melhuish and Gardiner) 60
suncream 64, 85
supply-side funding 19
sustainability 91, 113–14, *114*, 117, 118
Sylva, K. 60

T

table-top activities 80–1
tacit knowledge 66–71
tactile care 63
tactile deprivation 62–3
take-home teddies 87

Takeuchi, H. 66
'taking care of' 55–6, 118
tax-free childcare schemes 17
teachers and teaching 9, 46
technology 81, 82
terminology 4–8, 112
Theory X and Y perspectives 83
three-pillar model of sustainability 113–14, *114*
time 76–9
Tomkins, L. 54
touch 62–5
toys and equipment 87
training 25–7
transitions 5, 21, 40, 104
Tronick, Edward 65
Tronto, Joan C.
  care 6, 108
  'caring about'/'taking care of' 85
  challenges of democratic life 113
  ethical childcare 54–7
  four phases of care 37, 55–6, 117–18
  the market providing care 20
  Moral Boundaries **50**
  time and ethical care 78
troubled families 23
Tsoukas, H. 66, 70, 94, 95, **96–7**, 110–11
two-tier provision 42, 105–6

U

UK 16–18, 25, 29, 32
uncaring and exploitative organisations 34
unconscious attention 73
unconscious bias 52
unconscious caring habits 70
underfunding 2
  see also funding issues
undervaluing care 2, 7, 112
unethical practice 39, 102
uniforms 84
United Nations 10
unqualified staff 25
urban environments 91
US 29, 31

V

valorisation of education over care 8
values articulation 99–100
'values work' (Gehman) 98
Vygotsky, Lev **61**

W

Watkins, Gloria (bel hooks) 76
Weick, Karl 93
wet flannel training 26–7, 64
whole-group learning 26–7
Winnicott, D. 51
women 2, 46, 48

Index

'women's intuition' 47
woodland 18
word clouds 88, *89*
World Health Organization 71
'Wraparound care' 23
wrong turns in care 2–4
Wuori, Dan 7, 31–2

Y

younger employees 28

Z

Zeedyk, Suzanne 5, 81
zero-hours contracts 17

www.ingramcontent.com/pod-product-compliance
Lightning Source LLC
Chambersburg PA
CBHW071714020426
42333CB00017B/2267